Dear student,

Green Line Oberstufengrammatik – Arbeitsheft is the perfect companion to your grammar reference book *Green Line Oberstufengrammatik*. Both books have the same structure – a glance at the tables of contents confirms that the chapters in the reference book and the *Arbeitsheft* are the same.

During your last two to three years at school when you are preparing for your final exam, you will come across points of grammar that you are either unsure of or where you constantly make mistakes. In these cases you can consult your reference book, either via the chapter headings or by using the index *(Register)*.

The *Arbeitsheft* contains exercises that correspond exactly to the paragraphs in *Green Line Oberstufengrammatik*. The levels *Basisniveau* and *Aufbauniveau* are also adhered to. Next to the heading of each exercise is a note about which paragraphs it covers. Occasionally the content covers more than one paragraph from the chapter. In these cases read every paragraph covered by an exercise before you do it.

The answers to each exercise can be found on the CD-ROM at the back of the book. Put it into your computer and it should start automatically. (If it doesn't, look at the instructions on the page where you found the CD-ROM.). The simple, clear navigation leads you quickly to the answers. Each exercise has its own pdf document with answers and comments to help you to understand why your answer is right – and more importantly if yours is wrong, why. If these comments are not enough, the references there to the chapters in the reference book will show you where you can find more detailed information.

If you work through a whole chapter or whole chapters in the reference book, you can also work on whole sequences of exercises in the *Arbeitsheft*. At the end of each section A, B and C there is a small chapter with exercises covering the content of that section. These chapters are called *Focus* and each exercise deals with several grammar points. These exercises can also be used to find out which grammar needs your special attention.

The last part of the book, section *D Review*, provides a series of exercises containing grammar from all of *Green Line Oberstufengrammatik*.

We wish you every success with your efforts to improve your grammar and in your final exams,

Your *Green Line Oberstufe* Team

Symbolerklärung

→G25 Look at this paragraph in *Green Line Oberstufengrammatik*.

→K8 Look at this chapter in *Green Line Oberstufengrammatik*.

Inhaltsverzeichnis

A Zeitformen

B Zusammenhänge herstellen

C Beschreiben und benennen

D Review

A Zeitformen

1 Gegenwärtiges ausdrücken

Grundniveau

1 Simple present and present progressive →G1–G3

Decide which form is most suitable in these short dialogues. There are not always signal words to help you and some sentences contain questions and negative forms!

a) At the breakfast table

Dad: Listen to this, darling. The paper ________ (say) that children who ____________ (get up) early ________ (do) better at school.

Mum: ________________________ (you really believe) what the papers say?

Dad: Yes, of course. Look at our kids! They ____________ (do) very well at the moment.

Mum: Maybe that's because they ____________ (always go) to bed early, too.

b) At the computer store

Alex: Good morning, Mr Felton. John has just called in sick so we need a substitute.

Mr Felton: Let me see. – Ben ____________ (not work) on Tuesdays and Dave ____________ (help out) in our West End branch. What about Steve?

Alex: Oh no, not Steve. He is a good technician but he ________ (hate) working in the store. He ____________ (never find) the right words for customers. Sally could help us, though.

Mr Felton: No, I need her in the office. We ____________ (deal) with the emails and online orders. Let's call Ben. He ____________ (work) at home today so he can be here in 20 minutes.

Alex: I hope so! A lot of people ________________ (already wait) downstairs. The queue ________ (grow) longer and longer and the customers ________________ (become) more and more impatient.

c) At the university

Student: Excuse me, I ____________ (look) for Dr Jones. I'm in the workshop on Romantic Poetry that he ____________ (do) this term and I ____________ (desperately need) to talk to him about my paper.

Secretary: I see. I'm afraid Dr Jones ____________ (not have got) student counselling today.

Student: That's a bit of a nuisance. ____________ (you know) where I can find him now?

Secretary: Let me have a look at his timetable. On Mondays his first seminar ____________ (start) at 10:15, and the next one is at 13:15. So he ____________ (probably have) lunch right now. Maybe you'll find him in the cafeteria.

Student: Thank you very much!

d) In the kitchen

Sam: I ____________ (try) to contact Tom. ____________ (you know) where he is?

Nikki: Yes, he ____________ (spend) a few days in Scotland. He ____________ (prepare) for his final exam.

Fiona: Typical. Tom ____________ (always leave) things like that to the last minute. He ____________ (go) to parties, ____________ (play) football, ____________ (do) a million other things and ____________ (not think) about the exams at all.

Nikki: Yes, so that's why he ____________ (take) a few days off now.

Sam: Well, I ____________ (wonder) if it's enough. When you ____________ (take) an exam, you ____________ (need) more than a few days' preparation.

2 Stative verbs – Stative and dynamic use →G4, G5

Translate the following sentences, overheard from telephone conversations. Use the verbs given.

1. Ich probiere gerade eine Auswahl Weißweine. Der Chardonnay schmeckt hervorragend. (taste 2x)

____

____

2. Ich höre dich im Moment sehr gut – du brauchst nicht zu schreien. (hear)

____

____

3. John ist gerade nicht da – aber warte eine Sekunde – ich höre gerade, wie jemand die Treppe heraufkommt. (hear)

____

____

4. Mein kleiner Bruder ist in der 7. Klasse, und er ist gerade sehr schwierig. (be 2x)

____

____

5. Was meinst du mit „Ich kann nicht kommen“? Ich zähle auf dich! Du weißt doch, wie viel das Projekt für die Prüfung zählt. (count 2x)

____

____

6. Ich habe keine Ahnung, wie kalt es draußen ist. Ich nehme gerade ein Bad. (have 2x)

____

____

7. Ich denke über ein neues Auto nach. Was meinst du? (think 2x)

____

____

8. Triffst du dich noch mit John? … Oh, ich verstehe. Wie schade – er sieht wirklich gut aus! (see 2x)

____

3 Summary – Sequence of tenses →G6

a) *Read the text. The notes on the right will help you to complete the task below.*

The Story of an Hour

Knowing that Mrs. Mallard was afflicted with a heart trouble, great care was taken to break to her as gently as possible the news of her husband's death.
It was her sister Josephine who told her, in broken sentences; veiled hints that revealed in half concealing. Her husband's friend Richards was there, too, near her. It was he who had been in the newspaper office when intelligence of the railroad disaster was received, with Brently Mallard's name leading the list of "killed." […]
When the storm of grief had spent itself she went away to her room alone. She would have no one follow her. […]

1. Introduce the main character and the most important things that happen in one or two sentences – mind the sequence of events!

She could see in the open square before her house the tops of trees that were all aquiver with the new spring life. The delicious breath of rain was in the air. In the street below a peddler was crying his wares. The notes of a distant song which some one was singing reached her faintly, and countless sparrows were twittering in the eaves. There were patches of blue sky showing here and there through the clouds that had met and piled one above the other in the west facing her window. […]

2. Use her impression of the surroundings as the background of her inner development.

She was young, with a fair, calm face, whose lines bespoke repression and even a certain strength. But now there was a dull state in her eyes, whose gaze was fixed away off yonder on one of those patches of blue sky. It was not a glance of reflection, but rather indicated a suspension of intelligent thought.
There was something coming to her and she was waiting for it, fearfully. What was it? She did not know; it was too subtle and elusive to name. But she felt it, creeping out of the sky, reaching toward her through the sounds, the scents, the color that filled the air.

[…] When she abandoned herself a little whispered word escaped her slightly parted lips. She said it over and over under her breath: "Free, free, free!" […]

She did not stop to ask if it were or were not a monstrous joy that held her.
A clear and exalted perception enabled her to dismiss the suggestion as trivial.

She knew that she would weep again when she saw the kind, tender hands folded in death; the face that had never looked save with love upon her, fixed and gray and dead. But she saw beyond that bitter moment a long procession of years to come that would belong to her absolutely. And she opened and spread her arms out to them in welcome.

There would be no one to live for during those coming years; she would live for herself. There would be no powerful will bending hers in that blind persistence with which men and women believe they have a right to impose a private will upon a fellow-creature. […]

Her fancy was running riot along those days ahead of her. Spring days, and summer days, and all sorts of days that would be her own. She breathed a quick prayer that life might be long. It was only yesterday she had thought with a shudder that life might be long.

3. Describe her inner development – as opposed to the first impressions the reader gets – depict her final state of mind clearly!

She arose at length and opened the door to her sister's importunities. There was a feverish triumph in her eyes, and she carried herself unwittingly like a goddess of Victory. She clasped her sister's waist, and together they descended the stairs. Richards stood waiting for them at the bottom.

Someone was opening the front door with a latchkey. It was Brently Mallard who entered, a little travel-stained, composedly carrying his grip-sack and umbrella He had been far from the scene of accident, and did not even know there had been one. He stood amazed at Josephine's piercing cry; at Richards' quick motion to screen him from the view of his wife.

But Richards was too late.

When the doctors came they said she had died of heart disease – of joy that kills.

4. Concentrate on the action! Which explanations must be provided – which tense must be used?

Kate Chopin, 1894

b) *Summarise* The Story of an Hour *in about 120–150 words. You might find the clues provided helpful.*

1. ______

2., 3. ______

4. ______

4 The sequence of tenses – Mediation →G6

Read these German film reviews and mark the points you find most important. Then write summaries of the reviews in English, using the present tense sequence. You may need a dictionary.

Filmreview | Rubbeldiekatz

Rubbeldiekatz Inhaltsangabe

Ein Job ist ein Job, sagt sich der erfolglose Theaterschauspieler Alexander (Matthias Schweighöfer), verwandelt sich in „Alexandra", schlägt alle Konkurrentinnen aus dem Feld und ergattert tatsächlich eine Frauenrolle in einem großen Hollywoodfilm! Aber kann er in Pumps und ausgestopftem BH auf Dauer überzeugen? Mehr als ihm lieb ist! Sein Kollege (Max Giermann) beginnt ihn zu begrabschen, auch der genialische Regisseur (Joachim Meyerhoff) findet ihn unwiderstehlich, Alex' Ex-Freundin (Susanne Bormann) flippt aus und seine ruppigen Brüder (Detlev Buck, Maximilain Brückner) und deren durchgeknallter Kumpel (Denis Moschitto) mischen das Filmset auf. Alex würde seine falschen Locken am liebsten an den Nagel hängen, wenn es nicht längst zu spät wäre – er hat sich unsterblich in seine Partnerin verliebt: Superstar Sarah Voss (Alexandra Maria Lara). Ist Alex Frau genug, um seinen Mann zu stehen?

Filmreview | Shanghai

Shanghai Inhaltsangabe

Mit „Shanghai“ ist Regisseur Mikael Hafström und Autor Hossein Amini ein faszinierender historischer Polit-Thriller gelungen, der den Blick auf ein bisher weniger beachtetes Kapitel des Zweiten Weltkriegs lenkt.
Shanghai 1941: Die Stadt ist die letzte Bastion in China, die sich gegen die japanischen Allmachtsphantasien zur Wehr setzt. Die Japaner bereiten von hier aus den Angriff auf Pearl Harbor vor und bekämpfen den chinesischen Widerstand gegen die Besatzung mit brutalen Mitteln. Gemeinsam mit den Nazis teilen sie die Welt untereinander auf. Als Japan- und Deutschland-treuer Journalist getarnt will der amerikanische Agent Paul Soames (John Cusack) den Mord an einem guten Freund aufklären. Er gerät dabei immer tiefer in ein undurchsichtiges Netz aus Intrigen und nationalstaatlichen Interessen in der in Zonen aufgeteilten asiatischen Metropole.

Filmreview | Männer, die auf Ziegen starren

Männer, die auf Ziegen starren (The Men Who Stare At Goats) Kritik

Nicht immer ist es einem Filmkritiker vergönnt, einen einfach nur schlechten Film zu sehen. Manchmal muss man sich mit unglaublich schlechten Filmen quälen. So zum Beispiel „Männer, die auf Ziegen starren“ mit unzähligen Stars, die im Film ihr Talent vergeuden, wie ich es bisher nur von Cohen-Filmen kenne.
Da geht es also um eine Spezialeinheit, die mit Gänseblümchen und Tanz versucht, die Welt besser zu machen. Denkt man in den ersten Minuten noch, dass sich etwas annähernd Interessantes entwickeln könnte, wird man einen Sekundenschlaf später ins langweilige Leben zurückgerissen. Ewan McGregor – für mich der einzige Höhepunkt – erzählt als Bob Wilton aus der Ich-Perspektive, wie er auf die Jedi-Krieger stößt und somit die Story seines Lebens verfasst. Mag sein, dass Anspielungen auf Star Wars und diverse andere Kultfilme funktionieren und im extremsten Falle auch zünden, aber wenn ich lediglich Gags ohne Zusammenhang sehen möchte, schalte ich die nächstbeste Comedy-Sendung ein.

5 Present tense sequence – Error spotting →G6

Read this text about a famous scene from Shakespeare's Macbeth. Some of the verb forms are marked. Decide if they are right or wrong and correct them if necessary.

In the famous banquet scene Shakespeare **has displayed** (1) his art most skillfully.
Macbeth and his wife are about to start the banquet when one of the murderers **is informing** (2) Macbeth that Banquo **had been killed** (3) but his son Fleance **has escaped** (4). When Macbeth is asked to sit among his nobles he discovers the bloody ghost of Banquo, who **is sitting** (5) in his place.
While the other guests **enjoyed** (6) themselves, Macbeth is shocked and **won't realise** (7) at first that he is the only one who can see the ghost.
The ghost disappears and Lady Macbeth **will manage** (8) to calm her husband down.
When the ghost **has re-appeared** (9) Macbeth is horrified again and this time Lady Macbeth **is sending** (10) away their guests who **have been** (11) worried about Macbeth.
In the end, when Macbeth **had recovered** (12), he reveals his suspicions about Macduff, who **doesn't come** (13) to the banquet, and he talks about his plan to visit the weird sisters again.
This scene both horrifies and fascinates the audience at the same time. It **has marked** (14) a turning point in Macbeth's fate as from now on things **are taking** (15) a turn for the worse.

1. ______________________
2. ______________________
3. ______________________
4. ______________________
5. ______________________
6. ______________________
7. ______________________
8. ______________________
9. ______________________
10. ______________________
11. ______________________
12. ______________________
13. ______________________
14. ______________________
15. ______________________

Aufbauniveau

6 The present tenses – Special use I →G7

Decide which of the given options is most suitable to fill the gaps.

1. I can't stand it any more. You ______________________ my CDs in the wrong cases.
   a) always put b) are putting c) are always putting

2. We've got plenty of time. The train ______________________ at 9:45.
   a) is leaving b) leaves c) is going to leave

3. My dad loves old records! He ______________________ them from a little shop in Chelsea.
   a) is getting b) always gets c) is always getting

4. I don't mind the bad weather here. We ______________________ to Spain next Friday.
   a) go b) are going c) are gone

5. You will learn a lot if you ______________________ this exercise.
   a) are doing b) do c) will do

6. Why ______________________ me with your computer problems. That's Steve's job.
   a) are you always bothering b) do you always bother c) are you bothering

7. Hurry up! Last admission ______________________ at 8:00!
   a) will be b) is going to be c) is

8. If the bus ______________________ soon, we'll miss our train.
   a) isn't turning up b) doesn't turn up c) won't turn up

7 The present tenses – Special use II →G7

Translate the following sentences into English.

1. Sie werden nächste Woche das Haus renovieren.

____

2. Wenn die Pläne der Bahngesellschaft realisiert werden, wird die Zugfahrt von London nach Birmingham nur 90 Minuten dauern.

____

____

3. Der letzte Bus kommt nach Mitternacht an und der erste Zug am nächsten Morgen fährt um 8:30 ab.

____

____

4. Jetzt bist du einfach albern!

____

5. Dauernd sagst du ihm, dass er alles falsch macht! Ich finde es so unfair.

____

6. Sie machen an Weihnachten immer ein großes Fest.

____

7. Nächstes Jahr fangen die Osterferien Mitte April an.

____

8. Wenn du nicht zu viel versprichst, werden die Leute nicht so viel von dir erwarten.

____

9. Am Wochenende beginnt die Vorstellung um 19:30.

____

10. Nächstes Jahr gehen sie wieder auf Tournee.

____

2 Vergangenes ausdrücken

Grundniveau

1 The rock concert – Simple past and past progressive →G8, G9

Choose between the simple past and the past progressive.

When we ______________ (arrive) at the arena the doors ______________ (be) still closed and about a hundred people ______________ (wait) to get in. Vendors ______________ (try) to tempt people into buying T-shirts and other merchandise. When we ______________ (finally go) into the auditorium, technicians ______________ (check) the sound and the lighting crew ______________ (test) the spots.
The show ______________ (be) due to start at eight o'clock, but at quarter past there ______________ (be) no sign of the band and people ______________ (still come) into the hall.
Twenty minutes later people ______________ (begin) to get impatient and ______________ (whistle) and ______________ (shout) when a tremendous blast of music ______________ (announce) the presence of the Moleskins on stage behind a black curtain.
By the time the band ______________ (start) on their second song, nobody ______________ (sit) on their seats any more and fans ______________ (dance) in the aisles.
Well into the second half of the concert, lead singer Lennie Mole ______________ (say) the band had a special guest that evening and ______________ (point) to a figure who ______________ (stand) in the shadows at the side of the stage. A spot ______________ (turn) onto the special guest and ______________ (reveal) last year's "X-Factor" winner, Teena Trashe.

2 Simple past and present perfect →G8, G10

Translate the sentences into English. Choose between the simple past and the present perfect.

1. Sie waren noch nie in den USA.

____

2. Diese Partei ist seit über zehn Jahren an der Macht.

____

3. Diese Produkte sind letztes Jahr auf den Markt gekommen.

____

4. Früher kosteten Telefonate ins Ausland viel Geld.

____

5. Wann hat die Regierung ihre Mehrheit verloren?.

____

6. Hattest du schon die Masern?

___

7. Er ist sehr plötzlich gestorben.

___

8. Hast du die neue CD der Moleskins angehört?

___

3 Present perfect simple and progressive →G10, G11

Use the appropriate form of the verb on the right: the present perfect simple or progressive.

1. a) Have you ________ to Tom? – Yes, he says we can meet on Sunday. **speak**
   b) Have you ________ to Tom? – Yes, that's why I'm late.
2. a) She hasn't ________ William for five years but he's coming back to England next week. **see**
   b) She hasn't ________ William for a few weeks. I think they had a row.
3. a) I've ________ the cellar but I'll do the rest tomorrow. **clear up**
   b) I've ________ the cellar as you asked me to do.
4. a) Look what they've ________. – That's awful. Can you repair it? **do**
   b) Look what they've ________. – That's typical of children. They can amuse themselves for hours.
5. a) We haven't ________ very pleasant weather recently. **have**
   b) We haven't ________ any snow for over five years.
6. a) They have ________ events in the Middle East as part of their course. **follow**
   b) They have ________ events in the Middle East so they are well informed about what is going on.

4 Mixed exercise – Floods in Australia →G8, G10, G11

Überschwemmungen in Australien

Im australischen Bundesstaat New South Wales bedroht* eine Überschwemmung die Stadt Wagga Wagga und ihre 58,000 Einwohner. Bislang wurden rund 240 Häuser im Norden der Stadt beschädigt. Mehr als 9000 Bewohner wurden aufgefordert*, ihre Häuser zu verlassen und viele von ihnen haben sich Medienberichten zufolge vor drohenden Fluten in Sicherheit gebracht*. Rettungskräfte* retteten Flutopfer von den Dächern ihrer Häuser oder Autos und das Militär warf aus der Luft Lebensmittelpakete ab. Gestern rief der Regierungschef des Bundesstaates, Barry O'Farrell, für die Stadt den Ausnahmezustand aus.

Unterdessen gab das meteorologische Amt* eine Unwetterwarnung* für Sydney und die südliche Küste von New South Wales aus. Nach heftigen Regenfällen traten Flüsse über die Ufer* und setzten mehrere Straßen unter Wasser. In den vergangenen Tagen hatten nach Behördenangaben rund 5000 Menschen ihr Zuhause verlassen. Das Flutdrama forderte bislang zwei Todesopfer. Der Südosten Australiens verzeichnete* in diesem Jahr einen der regenreichsten Sommer der vergangenen Jahrzehnte.

Vor rund einem Jahr war der Bundesstaat Queensland bereits von riesigen Überschwemmungen heimgesucht* worden. Dabei wurden 35 Menschen getötet. Die Wassermassen überfluteten zehntausende Häuser und vernichteten riesige Flächen Ackerland. Anschließend fegte* der Monstersturm „Yasi“ über das Land und richtete* weitere große Schäden an.

* **bedrohen** – threaten; **auffordern** – call upon; **sich in Sicherheit bringen** – move to safety; **Rettungskraft** – rescue service; **das Meteorologische Amt** – Bureau of Meteorology; **Unwetter** – severe storm; **über die Ufer treten** – burst one's banks; **verzeichnen** – experience; **heimsuchen** – strike; **fegen** – sweep; **anrichten** – cause

Give a summary in English about the floods in Australia. Structure it like this:

- What does the article say about the situation in Wagga Wagga?
- What is the general situation in Eastern Australia?
- What happened about a year ago in Queensland?

Floods are threatening the town of Wagga Wagga in New South Wales.

The situation is a reminder of

5 Past perfect and simple past →G8, G12

Use the words to make sentences with suitable verb forms.

1. Good morning, – Mrs Brown. I – call – last week – about – advert – paper.
2. if – start – sooner – relief efforts, they – save – more lives.
3. last year – than ever before – sell – Japanese – more cars – worldwide.
4. when – president – walk into – conference, delegates – stand up – applaud.
5. Louise – tell – him – about – what – she – see – the day before.
6. I – be – sorry, I – could – not – go – your party. I – tell – you – I – be – busy – last weekend.

6 Mixed exercise – Significant cigarettes →G8, G9, G12

Lev has decided to leave his home in Eastern Europe and head for London to find work so he can support his mother and daughter back home. Use the simple past, past progressive or past perfect where appropriate.

On the coach, Lev ________________ (choose) a seat near the back and he ________________ (sit) huddled against the window, staring out at the land he was ________________ (leave): at the field of sunflowers scorched by the dry wind, at the pig farms, at the quarries and rivers and at the wild garlic growing green at the edge of the road.

Lev ________________ (wear) a leather jacket and jeans and a leather cap pulled low over his eyes, and his handsome face was grey-toned from his smoking and in his hands he ________________ (clutch) an old red cotton handkerchief and a dented pack of Russian cigarettes. He would soon be forty-three.

After some miles, as the sun ________________ (come) up, Lev ________________ (take) out a cigarette and ________________ (stick) it between his lips, and the woman sitting next to him, a plump, contained person with moles like splashes of mud on her face, ________________ (say) quickly: "I'm sorry, but there is no smoking allowed on this bus."

Lev ________________ (know) this, ________________ (know) it in advance, ________________ (try) to prepare himself mentally for the long agony of it. But even an unlit cigarette was a companion – something to hold on to, something that had promise in it – and all he could be bothered to do now was to nod, just to show the woman that he ________________ (hear) what she ________________ (say), reassure her that he wasn't going to cause trouble; because there they would have to sit for fifty hours or more, side by side, with their separate aches and dreams, like a married couple, smell the food and drink each ________________ (bring) with them, note the degree to which each was fearful or unafraid, make short forays into conversation. And then later, when they finally ________________ (arrive) in London, they would probably separate with barely a word or a look, walk out into a rainy morning, each alone and beginning a new life. And Lev ________________ (think) how all of this was odd but necessary and already ________________ (tell) him things about the world he ________________ (travel) to, a world in which he would break his back working – if only that work could be found. He would hold himself apart from other people, find corners and shadows in which to sit and smoke, demonstrate that he ________________ (not need) to belong, that his heart ________________ (remain) in his own country.

From: Rose Tremain, *The Road Home*, 2008

7 Mixed exercise – Explaining differences and errors →G8–G13

Follow the instructions in each task.

1. Explain the difference in meaning in German.

a) They have waited for this decision for a long time.
b) They have been waiting for this decision for a long time.

___

___

2. What is the difference between these sentences? Explain in German.

a) When she came home from work, Tom got dinner ready.
b) When she came home from work, Tom was getting dinner ready.

___

___

___

3. What is wrong in this sentence? Explain in German.

When he told them about it, nobody was believing him.

___

___

4. Is there something wrong in this sentence? Explain in German.

Just before they had left the house, Marie made a quick telephone call.

___

___

5. Explain the mistake in this sentence in German. What would be correct and why?

In 2001 Islamist terrorists have flown two planes into the World Trade Center.

___

___

6. Why is it possible to use the progressive form of think in the first sentence and not the second?

a) Derek had been thinking about Charlotte all morning.
b) Derek had thought Charlotte was avoiding him.

___

___

___

7. a) Why does this sentence sound strange, taken out of context?

Early in the morning Jane was leaving for London.

___

___

b) Continue the narration to create a context for the sentence.

___

8 Mixed exercise – Britain in turmoil → G8–G13

Find and mark the errors in the tenses in this text. Correct them in the spaces between the lines.

Britain in Turmoil

The nation, the police and the government have been shocked to the core by incidents in several cities all over England in August 2011, which they have not been anticipating. The TV news had shown scenes in which marauding juvenile gangs had run wild in the streets of London, Manchester and Birmingham and had stolen goods from broken shop windows while policemen looked on helplessly.

Apparently the riots were starting soon after a young man, aged 29 and a father of four, was shot in Tottenham, North London, a district suffering from high unemployment. People there at once were putting the blame on the police, who they have never got on with at the best of times.

A few days later, when the riots were spreading to cities like Birmingham, Liverpool and Manchester, people in Germany have asked themselves whether dissatisfaction with social and political developments could cause similar violence in cities like Berlin or Hamburg. Experts have argued that in the past young people were always liable to protest when they had the feeling that politicians have disregarded their interests.

An expert was commenting on the terror in English streets as follows: "I was always afraid of outbreaks of violence because of the increase in urban areas inhabited by ethnic minorities, by people who never had the chance of making a better life for themselves. They live on the fringes of a society which, a few decades ago, has decided to let them immigrate in huge numbers from countries like India, Pakistan or Iran. To be quite honest, it surprises me that Bradford, a powder keg of social unrest, was not yet struck by the movement."

Aufbauniveau

9 Before the meeting – The sequence of past tenses →G14

a) *Read the text and put in the correct form of the verb using the past tense sequence. You may need to use the passive.*

Bruce Nesbitt __________ (sip) his coffee appreciatively. Rosalind, his new secretary, certainly __________ (understand) about coffee. [...] Only the best __________ (be) good enough. And why not indeed? He certainly __________ (deserve) it. He __________ (be) fifty tomorrow, and __________ (work) his way up through the ranks of the company to become the youngest Chief Executive in its history. He __________ (start) as an office-boy and now he __________ (be) the big boss. Now he could look forward to another ten good years in control before 'retirement'. Then his reputation __________ (bring) him a string of directorships and profitable consultancies as an 'elder statesman' of the business world. Life __________ (be) good and __________ (get) better. His wife __________ (be) still an attractive woman and their son, Alistair, just twenty-one, __________ (get) engaged to the daughter of Lord Bentwich this very evening. A grand party at Claridges Hotel __________ (arrange) and ... that __________ (remind) him. [...] There __________ (be) still the seating plan to finalize. Then there __________ (be) the unpleasant bit of business with Jenkins to settle. Jenkins __________ (have to) go. [...]

Bill Jenkins __________ (look) at his haggard und unshaven face in the mirror of the staff toilets at the factory. He __________ (be) the factory manager. He __________ (stay) on until the early hours of the morning trying to get the figures to balance. But, whatever he __________ (do), the gap __________ (remain): an enormous hole down which, somehow, £ 50,000 __________ (disappeared). He __________ (suspect) that Alistair __________ (take) it but he could not prove it. [...] In the past few months he __________ (spend) more and more nights like this at the factory. And more and more bottles of malt whisky __________ (keep) him company, helping to soften the blow which he __________ (know) __________ (soon, strike) him. Strangely enough, he now __________ (feel) quite detached. His main worry __________ (be) for Margaret and his daughter Mandy. What __________ (become) of them if anything __________ (happen) to him? They __________ (have) a very big mortgage – there __________ (be) still £ 100,000 left to pay for the house. And there __________ (be) all the specialists' bills for Mandy too. He sometimes __________ (wonder) if she __________ (ever, be) like other children.

His watch alarm suddenly ________________ **(start)** to ring, to remind him of the morning meeting. At least Alistair Nesbitt, with his nasty smile, ______________________ **(not be)** there; he ________________ **(be)** off somewhere in town running around with that rich bitch he __________________________ **(marry)**. Bill ________________ **(run)** the electric razor over his chin and cheeks, ________________ **(comb)** his hair, __________________ **(straighten)** his tie and ________________ **(walk)** out bravely to face the day.

From: *Man Proposes* by Alan Maley, 1995

b) ***Now read the text again and answer the questions using the past tense sequence.***

1. From the perpective of his position in the company, describe Nesbitt's career.

____

____

2. What special event was planned for the evening?

____

____

3. Why was the following day important for Nesbitt?

____

4. How did he imagine his retirement?

____

____

5. What was the 'unpleasant bit of business' with Jenkins?

____

6. Why was Bill Jenkins still in the factory?

____

7. Why wasn't it unusual for him to be in the factory so early in the morning?

____

____

8. What was the problem with the figures?

____

9. What were his suspicions?

____

____

10. What was the blow he was expecting?

____

11. Why was he worried about his family?

____

____

3 Zukünftiges ausdrücken

Grundniveau

1 Will future and going-to future →G15, G16

Read the following sentences. Explain in German the difference in meaning by pointing out in which situation the sentences might be used.

1. a) I'm going to have the fish at the restaurant.

____

b) I'll have the fish, please.

____

2. a) There will be some heavy thunderstorms in some regions of the South.

____

b) There is going to be a heavy thunderstorm very soon.

____

____

3. a) I think I'll spend my holidays in Scotland this year.

____

____

b) I'm going to spend my holidays in Scotland this year.

____

____

4. a) Who are you going to marry, Paul?

____

____

b) Paul, will you marry me?

____

5. a) Johnny Depp will be present at the premiere of his new movie.

____

b) I'm going to see the premiere of Johnny Depp's new movie.

____

6. a) Slow down, or we'll have a crash!

____

b) Slow down, we're going to have a crash!

____

2 Mixed exercise – Life after school →G15–G18

Read the following text and underline the form that you think is most suitable.

Tanja from Germany has written an e-mail to her penpal in Manchester about her plans for the summer:

Hi Leonie,

When we **'ll graduate/graduate/are graduating** from school next week, a new chapter in my life **starts/will start/is starting**. First of all, my friends and I **are going/go** on holiday to Spain to relax and enjoy ourselves. We're really excited! Our plane **leaves/is leaving/will leave/is going to leave** early in the morning on August 2 and, hopefully, we **'ll arrive/arrive** home safe and sound two weeks later. As soon as I **will be/am/am going to be** back, I **have/will have/am having** to look for a flat in Münster. I have been accepted by the university, and so has Meike, my best friend. We **are living/will live/are going to live/live** in a flat together, because we found out it's cheaper than living in a hall of residence! Finding a flat **won't be/isn't/isn't going to be** easy, however, because many first year students **will look/look/are going to be looking** for somewhere to live. But my mind is made up: We **will find/are going to find/find/are finding** a flat – no matter what! Meike and I **are meeting/meet** in Münster on Saturday – I've talked to a landlady whose flat we found on the Internet and we **'re looking/look/will look** at it in the afternoon. Hopefully we **won't just hang/aren't just going to hang/aren't just hanging** around in one of the famous pubs once we **will live/live** there! But there **is/will be/is going to be** enough time to get to know the city first. The semester **is starting/will start/starts/is going to start** on October 11, and classes **don't/won't/aren't going to** start until a week later. I'm sure you want to know what the guys are like at our university, don't you? I **tell/'ll tell/'m going to tell** you as soon as I find out! And I **won't forget/don't forget/'m not forgetting** to invite you to come to Münster during spring break – you **are going to love/'ll love/love/'re loving** it! Anyway, I have to stop writing now – I **'ll see/'m seeing/'m going to see/see** Dirk in an hour – I want to teach him some basic steps for the dance at the graduation ceremony! ☺

But more about THAT in my next e-mail …

See ya! Tanja

3 The future progressive →G19

Translate the following sentences, using the future progressive.
After translating, explain (in German) what the future progressive means in the English translation. Write in your exercise book.

1. Morgen Nachmittag liege ich am Pool.
2. Keine Sorge. Nach dem Regen wird die Sonne wieder scheinen.
3. Werden Sie Bewerber zum Vorstellungsgespräch einladen?
4. Ich nehme mal an, ihr esst Truthahn zu Weihnachten.
5. In einem Jahr studiere ich schon Architektur.
6. *(Am Telefon:)* Du willst uns alles von deinem Urlaub erzählen? Wir besuchen dich doch nächstes Wochenende.
7. Behandeln wir dieses Semester Shakespeares Dramen?
8. Wir werden in unserem Ferienhaus wohnen.

4 Mixed exercise – Educating Rita →G15–G18

In this extract from a play, Rita, a young hairdresser, wants to improve her education by taking a literature course. Her tutor is Frank, an alcoholic university lecturer.

a) *Read the text and underline all the sentences that refer to the future.*

b) *Explain why the form is used in each case, paying special attention to the speaker's intention.*

Rita: When do you actually, you know, start teaching me?

Frank: *(looking at her)* What can I teach you?

Rita: Everything.

(Frank leans on the filing cabinet, drinks, shakes his head and looks at her)

Frank: I'll make a bargain with you. Yes? I'll tell you everything I know – but if I do that you must promise never to come back here ... You see I never – didn't actually want to take this course in the first place. I allowed myself to be talked into it. I knew it was wrong. [...] I'm sorry – there are other tutors – I'll arrange it for you ... post it on ... *(He looks at her)*

(Rita slowly turns and goes towards the door. She goes out and quietly closes the door behind her. Suddenly the door bursts open and Rita flies in)

Rita: *(going up to him)* Wait a minute, listen to me. Listen: I'm on this course, you are my teacher – and you're going to bleeding well teach me.

Frank: There are other tutors – I've told you ...

Rita: You're my tutor. I don't want another tutor.

Frank: For God's sake, woman – I've told you ...

Rita: You're my tutor.

Frank: But I've told you – I don't want to do it. Why come to me?

Rita: *(looking at him)* Because you're a crazy mad [...] artist who wants to throw his students through the window, and I like you. *(After a pause)* Don't you recognize a compliment?

Frank: Do you think I could have a cigarette?

Rita: *(offering the packet of cigarettes)* I'll bring my scissors next week and give you a haircut. ______________________

Frank: You're not coming here next week. ______________________

Rita: *(lighting his cigarette)* I am. And you're getting your hair cut. ______________________

Frank: I am not getting my hair cut. ______________________

Rita: *(getting her bag)* I suppose you want to walk around like that, do you? *(She goes towards the door)* ______________________

Frank: Like what? ______________________

Rita: *(getting her coat)* Like a geriatric hippie. ______________________

Willy Russell, *Educating Rita*, 1981

5 Mixed exercise – The future of human communication →G15–G19

Fill in the correct form of the verb in brackets to express future meaning. Choose between the will future, the going-to future, the simple present, the present progressive and the future progressive. Sometimes you will need to use the passive voice and the future in the past, too.

The future of human communication

In the last 30 years the world has seen a revolution in technology and communication: PCs have entered private homes and almost everyone has access to the World Wide Web. People communicate via e-mail, Skype and SMS rather than by landline phones or posted letters.

In 1980, who could have guessed that people ______________ (communicate) that way 30 years later? Most probably, human communication ______________ (be) totally different in 30 years' time, as human communication is constantly changing. It's almost certain that not far from now, no letters ______________ (write) on "real" paper and none ______________ (send) via traditional mail. If people ______________ (want) to send a handwritten letter, they ______________ (take) advantage of the new technology. In just a few years people ______________ (write) electronic letters on a pad by hand and ______________ (send) them to their mail delivery company. Once the letter ______________ (be) on the mail server, it ______________ (print out) and ______________ (deliver) on the same day – anywhere in the world!

In view of current developments, it is certain that not only writing but also how we read ______________ (change) enormously in the next few years: The Frankfurt Book Fair ______________ (open) its doors again in October, and this time it ______________ (present) an even larger number of books in electronic form. You ______________ (be able to) read them on an electronic book reader like the Kindle.

In the future you ______________ (say) to your friends, "I ______________ (take) ten books with me on holiday, and I ______________ (still have) enough space for all my clothes in the suitcase!"

All thanks to your electronic book reader which doesn't weigh more than a bar of chocolate.

Even if some people might not like these trends, soon they, too, ______________ (force) to open their mind to new ways of communication. Some companies nowadays, for example, don't have a call centre and the only way to contact them is to send an e-mail. Some think this ______________________ (lead) to impersonal customer care – a justified fear, as it seems. However, if enough people say they ______________________ (cancel) their contract with such a company because a competitor provides more personal customer service, then this trend towards communicating exclusively via electronic channels might be slowed down. However, it ______________________ (not stop) because, as we all know, the communications revolution is already underway.

6 Mixed exercise – Dave's calendar →G15–G19

Look at Dave's calendar for next week and do the tasks below, using appropriate forms for expressing the future from paragraphs 15 to 19.

MONDAY	TUESDAY	WEDNESDAY	THURSDAY	FRIDAY	SATURDAY	SUNDAY
10:30am Latin test (60 minutes) 5pm – 6pm Tennis with Dad	12:30pm Meet Sarah at school canteen for lunch afternoon Help Grandpa in the garden? (check again!)	Teachers' conference: free afternoon! ☺	9am Presentation for Biology class 7pm Meet Sarah at the cinema (maybe horror movie!?☺)	2:15pm Chester train (arr.: 15:02) (pack U2 tickets!!!) 3:15pm Meet Mike on platform 8 for London train	In London with Mike 8pm U2 concert (pack tickets!!!)	12:23pm Train back home early evening must do homework for Monday ☺

a) *Write a suitable sentence about Dave's week.*

1. Monday 10:45am ______________________
2. Thursday 9am ______________________
3. Saturday 8:30pm ______________________
4. Monday 5:30pm ______________________
5. Friday 2:15pm ______________________
6. Wednesday afternoon ______________________
7. Thursday 7pm ______________________
8. Saturday morning ______________________
9. Sunday evening ______________________
10. Sunday 12:23pm ______________________

b) *On the Sunday before Dave's busy week starts, he is talking to his mum.*
Mark the mistakes in expressing the future and correct them in the space on the right.

Mum: Well, Dave, lazy week ahead? ______

Dave: Actually, according to my calendar, I am quite busy. ______

Mum: Really? Why is that? Anything important on tomorrow? ______

Dave: Not really – I write a Latin test tomorrow morning, but I've revised ______
quite a bit, so I think I'm doing quite well. ______

Mum: Won't you play tennis with Dad tomorrow evening? ______

Dave: Of course, we always play on Monday evening in the summer. ______

Mum: By the way, my book club comes over on Tuesday afternoon. ______
Can you help me move the dining-room table? ______

Dave: Sorry, Mum. I think I'll help Grandpa in his garden. I must check with him. ______

Mum: Then you aren't going to meet my friends. They'd like to get to know you. ______
Maybe at the weekend then, when we … ______

Dave: Mum! I'm being in London with Mike for the entire weekend, ______
U2 will play at Wembley! ______

Mum: Oh, I forgot. What a pity … My friends really are very nice, you know. ______

Dave: Look, Mum, I promise I will be here when your club meets at our ______
house again. ______

Mum: So, what are your plans for the weekend, then? ______

Dave: Well, the train for Chester leaves at quarter past two, so I take the 1:45 bus. ______
At quarter past three I'm meeting Mike on platform 8 at Chester station ______
to catch the train to London. ______

Mum: Then you can use all of Saturday morning and afternoon to do some ______
sightseeing – that's going to be nice … See Buckingham Palace, the ______
Houses … ______

Dave: Mum! We'll see U2! It's U2, understand?! Mike and I won't be doing any ______
sightseeing! ______

Mum: Well, enjoy the concert. As you stay at your Aunt Mary's, ask her about her ______
plans for the summer and give her my love. And don't forget to thank her ______
for letting you stay. ______

Dave: No Mum, I don't forget, I promise. As soon as we'll get to her place, I will ______
say thank you to her for letting us sleep there, heh, heh, heh … ______

Mum: I told her you will go to church with her on Sunday morning. ______

Dave: I know, Mum, and I told Aunt Mary that we were so tired after the concert ______
that we don't get up before 11 o'clock. As our train will leave at 12:23, there ______
isn't any time for church. You may ask why I come home so early. Well, I ______
have some homework to do for Monday, so I don't want to get back too late. ______

Aufbauniveau

7 By the year 2012 – The future perfect simple and progressive →G20, G21

You have travelled back in time to the year 1792 and are talking to George Washington, the first president of the newly-founded United States of America.

a) *You want to tell him, from a 2012 point of view, about how America has developed. These matters are in the past for you but in the future from Mr Washington's point of view. Use the future perfect simple or future perfect progressive (active and passive).*

1. USA – expand – from Atlantic Ocean – Pacific

____

____

____

2. Thousands of people – immigrate – USA – every year

____

____

____

THE DIS-UNITED STATES—A BLACK BUSINESS.

3. it – fight – civil war –North and South

____

____

____

4. slavery – abolish – black people – give – vote

____

____

____

5. USA – enjoy – peaceful relationship with Canada – over two centuries

____

____

____

6. it – be involved in – two world wars – many conflicts – Asia – Middle East

____

____

____

7. it – become – most powerful nation – earth

____

____

____

8. Companies – pay – goods and services – US dollars – worldwide – over 60 years

____

____

____

9. New York – grow – huge city

____

____

____

10. USA – explore space – over 50 years

____

____

____

8 Other ways of expressing the future →G22

Complete the sentences, using the the option that is best suited to the intended meaning.

be unlikely to | be bound to | be yet to | be about to | be likely to | be certain to | be on the brink of | be due to

1. Don't argue with Dad any more. He looks as if he ______________________ explode!
2. You could still apply for this job. Applications ______________________ be sent in by the end of next week.
3. The revelation of the scandal means the Prime Minister's days are numbered. He ______________________ resign later this week.
4. Everyone wonders what the President's response will be, but he ______________________ make an announcement.
5. Pete has really studied hard for his finals, so he ______________________ pass his exams.
6. They have had a long journey so when they arrive they ______________________ be hungry.
7. Well, he's just got divorced so I think he ______________________ be thinking about getting married again for some time.
8. The court ruled that the directors will be fined but the amount ______________________ be decided.
9. The Conservatives are so angry with the Liberal Democrats that they ______________________ dissolving the coalition.
10. At last fans of Robert Pattinson really do have something to look forward to. His latest film ______________________ be released next week.

4 Das Passiv verwenden

Grundniveau

1 Forms of the passive →G23, G24

Make passive sentences using the marked part of these active sentences as the subject.

1. The M25 between Junctions 20 and 24 has just been closed for eight hours.
   The police have advised drivers to use alternative roads.

   ____

2. The police hunt after a series of bank robberies in Sussex seems to be yielding initial results.
   The police have arrested two suspects and are holding them for questioning.

   ____

3. Farmers wonder why their fields are always covered with stones.
   The gravitational pull of the moon is continually drawing materials from the earth's interior to the surface.

   ____

   ____

4. A Russian ship capsized off the Welsh coast in a blizzard last night.
   Prince William himself piloted the helicopter which rescued the Russian sailors.

   ____

5. When a lorry was checked by border control in Dover, the driver was in for a surprise.
   A gang had hidden a load of illegal drugs on the lorry while the driver was asleep.

   ____

6. The English think they scored a third goal in the 1966 World Cup final while the Germans think they did not.
   People will continue to talk about this controversial goal.

   ____

7. The credit crunch and a weak European currency are a threat to the banking system.
   The European Central Bank (ECB) will have to account for the dramatic losses incurred last month.

   ____

8. Mary can see the O_2 Arena from the bedroom of her Docklands flat.

   ____

2 The use of the passive – Signs →G24

What information do these signs communicate? Transform active constructions into passive ones and vice versa.

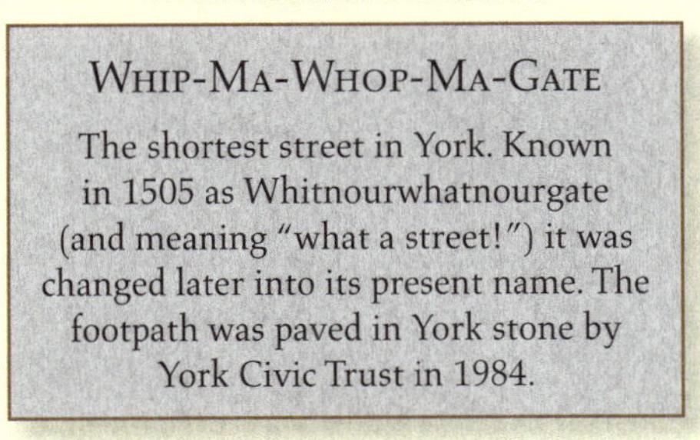

1. The seagulls should not/are not to … Chips should not …

2. Be careful … or you … be/get …

3. a) Cars must not …
   b) Passengers …

4. a) Bicycles should/must not …
   b) The authorities will … anything which …

5. a) In 1505 the citizens of York called …
   b) Later they …
   c) York Civic Trust … in 1984

6. What are the regulations for workers on this site?

3 The personal passive →G25

Rewrite the sentences, using a personal passive where possible.

1. Didn't they show you the sights of the city?

___

2. They still deny women the right to vote in quite a few countries.

___

3. People are likely to talk about her all over town.

___

4. They gave me a salary increase after two months and they have promised me a bonus at Christmas.

___

___

5. They didn't offer John enough money for his memoirs.

___

6. Someone may give him the advice he needs.

___

7. Nobody would have stared at her if someone had told her what to wear at the reception.

___

8. Never before has anyone spoken to me like that.

___

4 The use of the passive – Translation →G24, G25

Translate into English using passive sentences, also for the German "man/jemand".

1. Als Familie Davis aus dem Urlaub in Spanien zurückkam, überbrachte man ihnen am Flughafen schlechte Nachrichten. „Jemand ist in Ihr Haus eingebrochen und hat alles stark beschädigt".

   When the Davises returned home from their holiday in Spain, ___

   ___

   ___

2. Sofort fragte Mr Davis: „Kann man noch im Haus wohnen? Hat man die Einbrecher schon verhaftet?"

   Mr Davis asked immediately, ___

   ___

   ___

3. Man riet ihm, geduldig zu sein. „Die Polizei hat eine junge Frau in Gewahrsam *, die ständig verhört wird".

   ___

   ___

   ___

   ___

*in Gewahrsam haben – hold in custody

4. Auf dem Polizeirevier wurde die Familie Davis über die weiteren Ermittlungen informiert. „Man hat Blutflecken* im Wohnzimmer entdeckt. Es ist davon auszugehen, dass man das Haus versiegeln* muss".

____

____

____

5. Mrs Davis wurde immer nervöser. „Ich verstehe nicht, warum man uns nicht ins Haus zurückkehren lässt. Ich will, dass jemand mir den Polizeibericht zeigt."

Mrs Davis became more and more nervous. "I don't understand ______________________

____

____

6. Man teilte ihr mit, dass man Kritik an polizeilichen Maßnahmen überhaupt nicht schätzte*. „Sie können den Bericht nicht zum Lesen bekommen".

____

____

____

7. Dann kam der Polizeichef ins Zimmer und sagte: „Problem gelöst. Die Verdächtige* verletzte sich als das Fenster eingeschlagen wurde. Wir haben also die Einbrecherin".

Then the Chief Inspector came into the room and said, ______________________

____

8. „Man kann nur hoffen", sagte Frau Davis, „dass jemand früher oder später etwas gegen die wachsende Kriminalität tut. Man kann sein Haus gar nicht mehr verlassen aus lauter Angst, dass* jemand einbricht."

____

____

____

5 Mixed exercise – Newspaper articles →G23–G25

a) *You have interviewed different people about an incident involving a school bus. Use your notes to write an article for your local newspaper in your exercise book. Use passive forms where appropriate. Try and find a catchy headline for the whole article.*

- They have sacked the driver of a school bus.
- A teenager caught him on camera doing a Sudoku while driving children to school. He took the photo with his mobile phone.
- You can see the driver balancing a puzzle book on his steering wheel in the picture
- You can see him filling in the answers with a pen while driving in early morning traffic.
- Buses can cause a lot of damage and injuries in an accident.
- They have dismissed the driver, whom the police have not named, after his company launched an investigation.
- His company suspended him immediately. A disciplinary procedure followed. After that they made the decision to dismiss the driver.

*Blutflecken – bloodstains; versiegeln – seal; schätzen – appreciate; Verdächtige(r) – suspect; aus lauter Angst, dass – for fear that

b) *Use the appropriate passive constructions with the given verbs.*

Snow, ice and blizzards to hit Scotland and north of England this weekend

Parts of the UK ____________________ **(warn)** to batten down the hatches once again this weekend as a new wave of cold weather ____________________ **(forecast)** to hit the country.

Blizzards ____________________ **(predict)** across northern parts of the UK and the Met Office warns that Scotland ____________________ **(affect)** the worst of all.

The north and west coasts of Scotland are due to ____________________ **(hit)** by heavy snowfall and high winds, with the weather slowly moving inland.

Stephen Davenport, a senior meteorologist at MeteoGroup, explained that a blizzard ____________________ **(define)** as the combination of snow and winds of at least 25 mph. In this case, gusts of up to 60 mph ____________________ **(anticipate)**. "The brunt of the storm ____________________ **(bear)** by Caithness and Sutherland and eastern Aberdeenshire," he said. "The worst of the weather ____________________ **(expect)** to arrive at 9am this morning and will last until midnight, although its effects ____________________ **(still, feel)** well into tomorrow."

6 Mixed exercise – Cider making →G23–G25

This text is on the website of German cider maker. It's quite easy to understand but could do with the use of some passive constructions.

Rewrite the text in your exercise book so that it sounds more natural.

Generally people do not know that we produce high quality cider in Germany

- We grow the apples for our cider mainly in the southwest of Germany, where the climate is milder.
- We have to pick them at exactly the right time.
- We harvest our apples at the beginning of autumn.
- When we have picked them we cut them up in a special mill and then we have to press them at once.
- We keep the apple juice in old oak barrels for several months.
- We leave it there until it has developed its specific colour and flavour.
- We put it into one- and four-litre bottles before we sell it.

In pubs you can order our cider on draught or by the bottle. You can also buy it in many other European countries. May we remind you that you should consume alcohol responsibly.

And remember: You should rinse and return empty bottles to the shop where you bought your cider.

7 Mixed exercise – Use of the passive →G23–G25

In some of the sentences below it would be preferable to use the passive rather than the active.

Write OK after the sentences whose verb form does not have to be changed.
Rewrite the sentences whose verb form has to be changed and note the reason (A, B, C, D, E) for your decision.

A It is official: a rule, a code of behaviour.
B The agent is so obvious that it does not have to be mentioned.
C The agent is not known.
D It is preferable not to mention the agent.
E The subject clause is too long.

1. Everybody accepts that the man asks the woman to marry him.

____

____

2. Airport authorities have cancelled all flights due to adverse weather conditions.

____

____

3. Our president has decided to step down.

____

____

4. A burglar broke into my aunt's house last night.

____

____

5. The police officer who rescued widowed Gloria Deane's cat Ginger from drowning has inherited her estate.

____

____

6. Someone reported the incident to the police.

____

____

7. Those who had attacked the victim left him to die.

____

____

8. I love my pets and my pets love me.

____

____

Aufbauniveau

8 More complex forms of the passive →G26

a) *Complete the dialogues, using the appropriate more complex form of the passive. Choose between* **would be** **will have been** **would have been**

1. I need these books by tomorrow afternoon.
   – Don't worry, they ____________________ returned by then.
2. Look at all those people. It seems that anybody who could be possibly regarded as a celebrity is here today.
   – That's inflation for you! Ten years ago fewer people ____________________ invited to the ceremony.
3. This is a disgrace. The council still hasn't done anything about the holes in the road.
   – I know. A few years ago the damage ____________________ repaired at once.
4. Everyone knew the Trade Secretary's resignation was only a matter of time.
   – In fact, the President expected an announcement ____________________ made that afternoon.
5. There are always long queues for the river ferry during the tourist season.
   – This year will be different. The new bridge ____________________ opened by the summer holidays.

b) *Complete these dialogues, using a complex passive form and an appropriate verb.*

1. How did she get the results before everyone else?
   – Well, she found out they ____________________ at ten o'clock.
2. I need to know as soon as possible whether I can go on holiday in June.
   – Well, you can be certain a decision ____________________ before the end of the week.
3. I blame this awful weather on global warming. It just rains all the time.
   – That's true. In the past this period of rain ____________________ by sunny days.
4. So because of the mix-up, James's trip to India was uncertain up to the last minute?
   – Yes, he just hoped his visa ____________________ in time.

9 Further forms of the passive →G26, G27

React in the situations described in each sentence, using an appropriate passive form of the given verb.

1. You are looking at some old photos. In one you are on a beach and you think it's Tenerife. **take**
   ____
   ____
2. Mary's hair looks a lot different than when you last saw her. You ask her if she's been to the hairdresser's: **cut**
   ____
3. You plan to go on holiday to the USA but you notice that your passport has expired. **renew**
   ____

4. You arrive in your hotel room and find some clothes in the wardrobe. The previous guest probably forgot them. You call reception and tell the receptionist: **leave**

____

5. Your apartment is being renovated. The bedroom is next. **paint**

____

6. Mary has bought a new dress, which looks a bit too long. She hasn't got a sewing machine. It's really pretty, Mary. **shorten**

____

7. The parcel service has delivered some books you ordered from America. The package has a big stamp from customs on it. **open**

____

____

8. You and your friends are giving a party but you haven't got enough time to fetch all the drinks. **deliver**

____

10 Mixed exercise →G27, G28

Find the mistake(s) in each of these sentences and correct it/them.

1. My brother got his mobile phone steal in Rome.

____

2. Mary got fixed her nose last week.

____

3. We will try to have the exam results publish in the newspaper.

____

4. It's about time you had repaired your bike.

____

5. These presents will have to wrap before they can take to the party.

____

6. Has she had mowed her lawn?

____

7. These shirts are washed and ironed easily.

____

8. This bookshop never stocks books that are not sold well.

____

9. My mother's tomatoes and cucumbers need to water.

____

Focus A

1 Autobiographical investigations →K1–K4

In the following excerpt from William Boyd's latest novel some of the verbs are printed in bold letters. They cover many of the tenses available in English. Consult your grammar book and explain in each case in German why the tense chosen is appropriate.

It **is** the summer of 1900. I **am** fourteen years old and **am living** at Claverleigh Hall in East Sussex, the country seat of my stepfather, Lord Faulkner. My father **has been** dead for a year. My mother **married** Lord Faulkner nine months after my father's funeral. She's his second wife, the new Lady Faulkner. Everybody in the neighbourhood is pleased for old Lord Crickmay, a bluff*, kindly man in his late fifties, a widower with one grown-up son.

I still don't really know what I **feel** about this new arrangement, this new family, this new home. Claverleigh and this estate **remain** largely terra incognita. Beyond the two walled gardens there are woods and fields, copses* and meadows, paddocks* and two farms spread out across the downs* of East Sussex. It's a large well-run estate and I feel a permanent alien in it even though the servants in the house, the footmen, the housemaids, the coachmen and the gardeners, are all very friendly. They smile when they see me and call me "Master Lysander".

I **have been removed** from my school in London – "Mrs Chalmers' Demonstration School for Boys" – and **am being tutored** by the local curate, the Reverend Farmiloe, an old and learned bachelor. My mother tells me that, most likely, I **shall be sent** to a boarding school in the autumn.

It is a Saturday so I have no lessons but the Reverend Farmiloe **has asked** me to read a poem by Alexander Pope called "The Rape of the Lock". I **am finding** it very hard going. After lunch I **take** my book and **wander** out into the big walled garden, looking for a secluded bench where I can continue my laborious reading.

William Boyd, *Waiting for Sunrise*, London, 2012

is/am ______________________________

am living ______________________________

____

has been ______________________________

married ______________________________

feel ______________________________

remain ______________________________

smile/see ______________________________

have been removed ______________________________

____

am being tutored ______________________________

____

shall be sent ______________________________

____

has asked ______________________________

____

am finding ______________________________

____

take/wander ______________________________

*__bluff__ – schroff; __copse__ – Wäldchen; __paddock__ – Koppel; __downs__ – Hügelland; __secluded__ – abgelegen

2 Mediation – An interview at a university →K1–K4

You have applied for a place on a course at an English university and have gone there for an interview. Use the notes in German to answer the interviewer's questions.

Interviewer: Nice to see you. Did you have a good trip?

(gestern angekommen, schon eine Stadtrundfahrt gemacht)

____

Interviewer: Fine, so you have already seen some of the city. Why did you decide to apply to this university?

(wolltest immer in England studieren, seit der 5. Klasse Englisch = Lieblingsfach; Universität von einem Freund empfohlen, hat hier vor zwei Jahren einige Monate verbracht)

____

____

____

Interviewer: I see – but your application is not for Linguistics or English Literature; you would like to study Civil Engineering and Architecture – how come?

(Vater hat Baufirma* in Deutschland; hast vor, in dieser Firma zu arbeiten. Voraussichtlich auch Arbeit an Projekten in Südafrika und Australien, wirst dort vermutlich auch arbeiten müssen – Studium an einer englischen Universität sicherlich gut)

____

____

____

____

Interviewer: I see you have a clear idea about your future. Now, from your certificates I see that you did not take an advanced course in Chemistry. Don't you think Chemistry is necessary for a civil engineer?

(hast Physikkurs belegt, an der Schule Auswahl: entweder Chemie oder Physik. Information bekommen: an dieser Universität naturwissenschaftliche Kurse* für Ingenieure)

____

____

____

____

Interviewer: Yes, that's correct. It won't be easy, though. One last point. I see your English is quite good, but will you be able to follow lectures in English? And you will also have to pass an English test for foreign students.

(Hoffnung: dein Englisch gut genug fürs Studium. zurzeit Teilnahme an einer „Conversation Class" am British Council, im Sommer Praktikum* in Kapstadt geplant)

____

____

____

Interviewer: Thank you – that's all for today. Thank you for coming and have a safe trip home.

*__Baufirma__ – contruction company; **naturwissenschaftliche Kurse** – science courses; **Praktikum** – work placement

B Zusammenhänge herstellen

5 Einstellungen ausdrücken

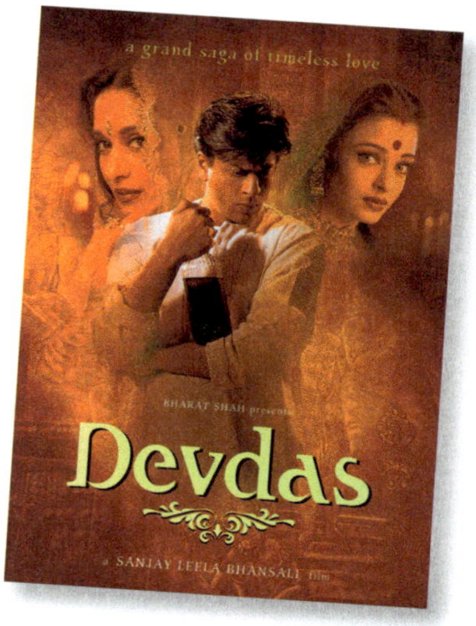

Grundniveau

1 Necessity and obligation I →G30

Rewrite the sentences so that they have the same meaning.
*Use **must, have to, have got to, need (to)** and add **not** where necessary.*

1. I strongly recommend that film. You will love it.
   You ______________________ see that film.
2. According to the law, everyone earning money is required to pay taxes.
   Everyone earning money ______________________ pay taxes.
3. Dr Thompson to a diabetic patient: "It is essential that you take your insulin. Forgetting it would have grave consequences."
   Dr Thompson: You ______________________ take your insulin.
   You ______________________ forget to take it.
4. Without a drastic decrease in expenditure, that company will soon be bankrupt.
   That company ______________________ decrease expenditure drastically.
5. Wearing glasses or contact lenses is necessary for people with poor eyesight.
   People with poor eyesight ______________________ wear glasses or contact lenses.
6. That sign tells drivers to wait for a signal before turning the ignition on.
   Sign: Drivers ______________________ wait for a signal before turning the ignition on.
7. "Is Friday the deadline for our history project, sir?" – "No, Monday will be OK."
   "______________________ we hand in our history project by Friday, sir?" – "No, you ______________________."
8. Being a sales representative means travelling a lot.
   A sales representative ______________________ travel a lot.

2 Necessity and obligation II →G30

Translate the German "müssen" in the most appropriate way. Write in your exercise book.

1. Wir werden uns beeilen müssen.
2. Der Motor muss noch nicht ersetzt werden.
3. Du musst dich unbedingt sofort anziehen.
4. Um die Katastrophenopfer zu retten, müssen die Behörden Sofortmaßnahmen ergreifen.
5. „Ich möchte Sie höflich daran erinnern, meine Damen und Herren, dass wir uns alle um neun Uhr in der Eingangshalle treffen müssen."
6. Musstest du an der Grenze deinen Pass zeigen?
7. Um sich vor Tropenkrankheiten zu schützen, müssen sich Touristen impfen lassen.
8. Laut diesem Schild neben dem Aufzug müssen die Hotelgäste im Brandfall die Treppe benutzen.

3 Permission →G31, G32

Fill in the gaps, using the various ways of expressing permission or absence of permission: ***may (not), to be (not) to, (not) to be allowed to, must not, can't/cannot****. Sometimes there is more than one correct solution.*

1. Passengers ______________________ use mobile phones and laptops during takeoff and landing but they ______________________ do so during the flight.
2. When you turn 18 next year, you ______________________ vote.
3. At my father's strict boarding school pupils ______________________ stay out after midnight.
4. In the library a sign says "Silence". Conversations ______________________ take place there.
5. I am sorry but you ______________________ enter the mosque wearing shoes.
6. We ______________________ forget that even leaders are only human.
7. Employers ______________________ discriminate against employees on any grounds.
8. In order to protect the informer, his identity ______________________ be revealed.

4 Permission and absence of permission →G31, G32

Translate the following sentences in your exercise book, basing your decision on the speaker's intention or the degree of politeness that is most appropriate.

1. Unbefugte dürfen dieses Gebäude nicht betreten.
2. Dürfte ich Sie zu Ihrem Tisch führen, mein Herr?
3. Wir durften in der Mathematikprüfung keinen Taschenrechner verwenden.
4. Studenten und Lehrkräfte dürfen in den Universitätsgebäuden nicht rauchen.
5. „Darf ich deine Kamera ausprobieren, Opa?" – „Nein, das darfst du nicht."
6. Dürfte ich eventuell kurz mit Ihnen sprechen, Herr Präsident?
7. „Denken Sie daran, Sie dürfen keine Wörterbücher in der Klausur benutzen."
8. *Student:* Dürfen wir das Fenster öffnen, Herr Professor?
   Professor Anderson: Nein, das dürfen Sie nicht.

5 Mixed exercise – Necessity and obligation, permission and absence of permission →G30–G32

Underline the expression best suited to the context. In some cases more than one is possible.

1. Football fans **must not/may not/are not allowed to** miss the semi-final next Saturday.
2. You must be crazy. You **may not/must not/can't** take a child into a striptease bar!
3. Dentist: You have a problem with gaps between your teeth.
   You **have to/must/can use** dental floss to ensure better hygiene.
4. "Should I take an umbrella?" – "No, you **must not/may not/needn't**.
   The forecast is good."
5. According to the law in this country, a voter **must/has to/needs to** be at least 18.
6. All applicants for this post **are to/must/should** send an updated CV and photo.
7. Civil servants in Germany **must not/can't/are not allowed to** go on strike.
8. I'm sorry, dear, but you **must not/can't/are not to** leave your tricycle here.
9. **May/Can/Might** I (just) make a suggestion, Mr Chairman?
10. Passengers **can't/are not to/may not** take more than one piece of hand luggage on board.

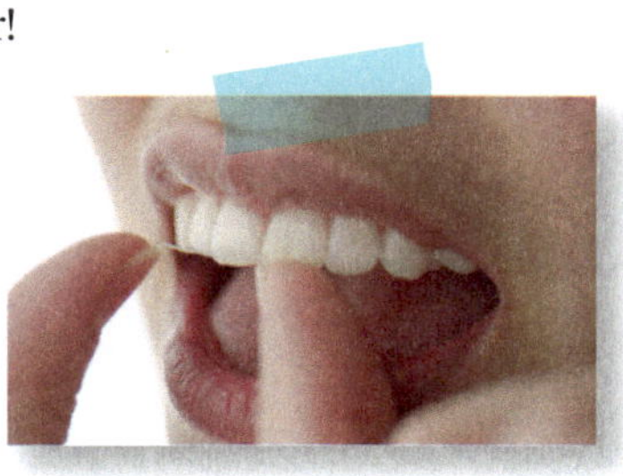

6 Ability and possibility →G33

Rephrase, using the various ways of expressing ability, possibility and probability and adding any verbs that are necessary. Sometimes more than one way of doing so is correct.

Example:
Cheetahs are the fastest runners on earth.
Cheetahs **can/are able to** run faster than any other species.

1. Have you been taught French? ______________________ French?
2. The divers managed to find the corpses of some of the passengers but they did not succeed in recovering the black box.
   The divers ______________________ the bodies of some of the passengers but they ______________________ the black box.
3. As late as the 19th century only relatively few poor people were literate.
   As late as the 19th century only relatively few poor people ______________________ .
4. Although his leg is in plaster, that won't prevent him from working.
   Although his leg is in plaster, he ______________________ .
5. It is possible to order a wide range of high-tech equipment from this online catalogue.
   A wide range of high-tech equipment ______________________ from this online catalogue.
6. Some astronomers believe in the possibility of life on other planets.
   Some astronomers believe that there ______________________ life on other planets.
7. Visitors to Antarctica will confirm that extremely low temperatures are possible there.
   Visitors to Antarctica will confirm that it ______________________ extremely cold there.

7 Asking for and giving advice →G34

Translate the sentences in your exercise book, using suitable ways of asking for and giving advice.

1. An deiner Stelle würde ich ihr verzeihen.
2. Bei solchem Wetter solltest du das Haus lieber nicht verlassen.
3. Sollte ich ein Jahr im Ausland studieren, was meinst du?
4. Ich finde, er sollte das Angebot annehmen.
5. Du solltest keine voreiligen Schlüsse* ziehen.

8 Requests and demands →G35

Complete the sentences using the modal best suited to the context from the list. Bear in mind the degree of politeness and the intention of the speaker. In some cases more than one of the modals is possible.

can | will | would | should | could

1. ______________________ be so very kind as to give the manager this document?
2. ______________________ greatly appreciate a prompt reply to our request.
3. ______________________ object to my using your mobile phone for an urgent call?
4. ______________________ check my Latin homework, Dad?
5. ______________________ post this letter on your way to school, darling?
6. When you have finished grading the exams, sir, ______________________ please let me know?
7. Your room is in a terrible mess. ______________________ tidy it up at once!

*voreilige Schlüsse – hasty conclusions

9 Mixed exercise →G36, G38

Put a cross × next to the right meaning of each sentence.

1. My annoying, super-cool cousin will insist on calling me a nerd.

☐ a) I don't like what my cousin does.
☐ b) I don't like my cousin.
☐ c) I'm not looking forward to my cousin's next visit.

2. When visiting a foreign country, people should respect its citizens' customs.

☐ a) I don't think people respect the customs in foreign countries.
☐ b) I am suggesting the right way to behave in foreign countries.
☐ c) There are rules about how to behave in foreign countries.

3. I'm afraid there is not much point in continuing the match in this downpour. We may just as well stop playing.

☐ a) I think we are allowed to stop playing.
☐ b) I think this is an annoying situation so let's stop the match.
☐ c) I want to suggest that we think about giving up.

4. Dad was furious, complaining bitterly that the airline could have informed him that his flight had been cancelled.

☐ a) Dad was angry because the airline had done something wrong.
☐ b) Das thought it was possible that the airline had called him.
☐ c) Dad was angry at the airline's poor customer service.

5. Paparazzi should not intrude on VIPs' private lives.

☐ a) I want to suggest the way paparazzi should behave.
☐ b) I think Paparazzi behave badly.
☐ c) I think what paparazzi do is wrong.

6. Could I offer you a cup of tea?

☐ a) I am offering you a cup of tea.
☐ b) I need your permission to make tea.
☐ c) Was it wrong that I didn't offer you tea?

7. You might at least offer to help me to carry these heavy bags.

☐ a) You didn't help me.
☐ b) You are behaving badly.
☐ c) I suggest that you help me.

8. Why didn't I take your advice? I should have listened to you.

☐ a) I think I'll listen to you in future.
☐ b) I have behaved badly and I'm sorry.
☐ c) I didn't take your advice and that was wrong.

9. I ought not to have stayed out so late before an exam. Instead of doing such a stupid thing, I should have had an early night.

☐ a) I sometimes behave badly but I know what to do in the future.
☐ b) I behaved badly but in future I will do the right thing.
☐ c) I did something wrong and I regret that I didn't do the right thing.

10. If you wish to save energy, you might consider the alternative of having solar panels installed.

☐ a) I think you made a mistake in the past.
☐ b) You are now allowed to install solar panels.
☐ c) I am making a suggestion about how to save energy.

11. The authorities have issued numerous avalanche warnings but some skiers simply won't pay heed.

- ☐ a) Some skiers refuse to listen to warnings.
- ☐ b) Some skiers aren't going to listen to any more warnings.
- ☐ c) Some skiers behave really stupidly about avalanche warnings.

12. George's essay was so ridiculously short that he might just as well have written nothing at all.

- ☐ a) I think George's work was very bad.
- ☐ b) I don't think George wrote an essay at all.
- ☐ c) I don't think George's essay was long enough.

10 Supposition – The McCann Method →G38

Read the following text and then fill in the gaps in the commentary, basing your decision on the information provided by the text. Choose from the following:

should/might/will | **won't *have/can't have*** | **may not have/might not have** | **could have/might have** | **must have/may have**

The McCann Method

Inspector Dick McCann is a brilliant detective, possibly the best in the whole of England. At any rate, he certainly has the best record of solving crimes all over Yorkshire. His colleagues joke that he obviously read lots of crime fiction in his youth.

The house key murder

There was a very mysterious case recently involving the murder of a wealthy elderly woman found strangled in her bed. The locked doors and windows in the house were intact so it had obviously not been entered by force. Moreover, nothing had been stolen. Her nephew Sam was the only other person to have a house key. However, he apparently had an alibi as he had been at a party organised by his local rugby club. On the other hand, he had a very strong motive because he was heavily in debt and his aunt, being childless, had promised to leave all her money to him. This motive and the key made him the prime suspect in spite of his alibi. McCann's team are now asking everybody who was at the party whether Sam was really there the whole time or whether it would have been possible for him to sneak away unnoticed in order to kill his aunt in cold blood. If they keep investigating long enough, the detectives expect ultimately to find evidence pointing to Sam's guilt.

Inspector McCann ______________ be the best detective in England. His colleagues joke that he ______________ read lots of crime fiction in his youth. But how does he do it? How did he use the McCann Method to solve "The house key murder"?

As the doors and windows at the scene of the crime were intact, the house ______________ been entered by force. The murderer ______________ had a key and ______________ wanted to steal anything. Theoretically, therefore, the old lady's nephew Sam ______________ been in her house that night. As Sam ______________ inherit his aunt's fortune, he ______________ ______________ been disappointed at her death. But if the other party guests were telling the truth, Sam ______________ stayed with them all evening. Consequently, if the many people who gave him an alibi are to be believed, he ______________ committed the crime. However, McCann, whose long experience has taught him to be sceptical about so-called watertight alibis, thinks Sam

__________________ sneaked away from the party unnoticed. After all, if he had then returned very quickly, they __________________ realized he had been absent. Thus, in view of the key and the strong motive, McCann's instinct has convinced him that Sam __________________ slain the unfortunate victim. Therefore, if all his most competent colleagues are involved in the investigation for long enough, it __________________ be possible to solve the crime.

11 The German "sollen" →G37, G39

Translate these sentences in your exercise book, making sure that you choose the most suitable equivalent of the German verb "sollen".

1. Dein Koffer sieht schwer aus. Soll ich ihn tragen?
2. Er hätte nicht so unhöflich sein sollen.
3. Der Umwelt zuliebe sollten wir uns eigentlich ein sparsameres Auto kaufen.
4. Grünes Gemüse soll viele Vitamine enthalten.
5. Gemäß ihrem Berufsethos* sollen Psychiater ihre Gespräche mit Patienten vertraulich behandeln.
6. Du solltest zu deinem Vorstellungsgespräch lieber pünktlich erscheinen.
7. Sollen wir deine Kollegen zu einer Grillparty einladen?
8. Eigentlich sollten wir die Arbeit bis gestern fertiggestellt haben.
9. Ihr Chef möchte Sie etwas fragen. Sie sollen sofort in sein Büro kommen.
10. Man sollte meinen, dass Zeitungsleser nicht immer so leichtgläubig* wären.

12 Mixed exercise – Modal mix-up →G30–G39

Our neighbour has been brushing up her English in preparation for a holiday in New Zealand.
For her English class she has prepared this little talk about her forthcoming holiday.
Unfortuately she has not quite mastered modal verbs yet.

Please correct her spectacular slip-ups. Underline the mistakes and write the correct sentences in your exercise book.

I am so looking forward to New Zealand.

I might have booked my flight earlier as it would have been cheaper that way, but I am relieved that I mustn't go through the hassle of applying for a visa. I have been warned that tourists don't have to import any raw meat, fruit or vegetables.

Unfortunately I won't be visiting Christchurch because there can be an earthquake like the one in 2011. Living in constant fear of earthquakes shouldn't be easy for its citizens. But I absolutely ought to visit Wellington and Auckland. 25 per cent of the population of Auckland is meant to be Asian. Is that true?

The scenery shall be breathtaking. It is well-known that the tracks in the bush might be very muddy all year round. I needn't forget to take waterproof walking boots with me. Everyone who has been to New Zealand says I simply could try white-water rafting. It's great fun! Do you think I ought try bungee jumping, too?

I would better buy a digital camera before I leave Germany.
If you are interested, I may give you copies of the best photos I take.

*__Berufsethos__ – professional ethics; __leichtgläubig__ – gullible

13 Mixed exercise – Hideouts or sacred places →G30–G39

Fill in the gaps, using the right modal verbs.

Hideouts or Sacred Places?

In Bavaria over 700 tunnel networks known as Erdställe have been found so far but as yet nobody has been ______________________ to say what purpose they served. In local dialects they are also known as "goblin holes" and are ______________________ to have been built as homes for helpful goblins.

Some of the tunnels are relatively large, so that adults ______________________ walk through them but they ______________________ stand up erect; they ______________________ bend over. Others are so small that explorers ______________________ crawl through them.

There are many theories concerning the function of these mysterious tunnels. For example, some local historians speculate that they ______________________ been used by Teutonic tribes seeking shelter in winter, but that ______________________ be true because they were too narrow, cold, damp and airless. There ______________________ be a more convincing explanation than that.

Another theory is that they ______________________ served as places where people ______________________ take temporary refuge from marauders. An argument in favour of this is that many tunnels doors have bolting devices which ______________________ be used only from within. Furthermore, as the passages were so narrow and winding, potential intruders would ______________________ move only in single file and would ______________________ crawl slowly, which would have made a successful attack virtually impossible.

The third theory is that the Erdställe served as symbolic empty graves for the souls of ancestors whose bodies the medieval settlers ______________________ leave behind. These "soul chambers" provided temporary accommodation where the souls ______________________ wait for Judgement Day.

Another argument in favour of a religious function is the fact that the cessation of Erdstall construction coincided with the emergence of the concept of purgatory in the late 11th century. This development ______________________ played a role. In fact, the absence of any written record of Erdställe shows that the Church ______________________ wanted attention drawn to this strange phenomenon.

Radiocarbon dating has proven that the tunnels ______________________ been built between 800 and 1,000 years ago. So far scientists ______________________ determine the age of some charcoal and various artefacts found. As only about 10 per cent of the Erdställe have been discovered to date, explorers and researchers ______________________ be kept very busy trying ultimately to shed more light on a great European puzzle.

Aufbauniveau

14 Semi-modal verbs →G41

Rewrite these sentences in your exercise book, using the modal verb form.

Example: Students **didn't use** to work so hard.
Students **used not** to work so hard

1. The government did not dare to raise taxes immediately before the elections.
2. You do not need to pay back the loan in the near future.
3. Grandma didn't use to be so forgetful.
4. Does this sentence need to be translated?
5. Did most men really use to believe that women were intellectually inferior?
6. Do backbenchers often dare to vote against their party leaders' decisions?
7. The pupils don't dare even to whisper in Mr Pascoe's history lessons.
8. She says that I frequently tell lies. What a cheek!

15 Other ways of expressing modality →G42

Use adjectives, adverbs and verbs to express the same ideas as in the sentences with the modal verbs.

Example: We **must** act immediately.
Immediate action **is necessary/essential**.

1. Don't wait for me. I may be late.
   Don't wait for me. I will ______________________.
2. As Daniel's qualifications are excellent, he ought to be offered the post.
   As Daniel's qualifications are excellent, he will ______________________.
3. The guide says walkers must not leave the signposted route.
   The guide ______________________.
4. People may not smoke on these premises.
   People are ______________________.
5. According to the latest statistics, the economic situation may be gradually improving.
   According to the latest statistics, the economic situation ______________________.
6. Economists think that exports should increase next year.
   Economists ______________________.
7. In fact, exports may even increase by up to 4 per cent.
   In fact, an increase ______________________.
8. Judging by his house, cars and clothes, he must be very wealthy.
   Judging by his house, cars and clothes, it is ______________________.
9. If you accept that executive position, you will have to move to Birmingham.
   Accepting that executive position will ______________________.
10. His parents said that he had to clean and tidy up his bedroom.
    His parents made ______________________.
11. Her mother is said to read all her e-mails.
    ______________________ reads all her e-mails.

6 Äußerungen wiedergeben

Grundniveau

1 Changing pronouns and adverbs of place and time – A telephone conversation →G43

Sally and Lisa's grandmother from Bristol is going to visit them in London at the weekend. Lisa is talking to her on the phone. Sally is standing next to her but can't hear what their grandmother is saying, so Lisa has to tell her sister everything.

Write Lisa's mediating part in the conversation. Change pronouns and adverbs of place and time where necessary.

Grandma: I'm really looking forward to seeing you again. It's been months since I last saw you.

Lisa (to Sally): ____

____

Sally: Tell her that we want to go to the London Arts Festival with her when she's here and that I bought the tickets this morning. This is one of my favourite festivals.

Lisa (to Anne): ____

____

____

Grandma: I'm delighted! Afterwards we might go to that nice restaurant where you, Lisa, first told me about your idea of studying in Germany for a year … Those salads they have there are really delicious! I can't remember the name …

Lisa (to Sally): ____

____

____

Sally: She means *Ye Olde London*. Tell her to bring her warm jacket – they say it will be cold here this weekend … Ask her what the weather is like with her.

Lisa (to Anne): ____

____

____

____

____

____

Grandma: OK, I'll bring some warm clothes. Well, I have to stop talking to you now. The sun is shining here at the moment so I'm going for a walk with my neighbour, Dorothy. Bye for now, I'm so happy that I'll be seeing you both on Friday!

Lisa: OK, bye, Grandma! (hangs up; to Sally:) ____

____

____

2 The backshift of tenses – A police report →G43–G46

The following statement was made to a police officer by a woman who witnessed a car accident. The next day the police officer has to write a report on the accident, based on the witness's statement.

Use the backshift of tenses and change pronouns and adverbs of place and time where necessary. Use different introductory verbs to avoid making the report sound too monotonous.

Statement by Mrs Julia Watson:

I was sitting in the café opposite the library. I was talking to my sister because we hadn't seen each other since last Monday and we wanted to spend our lunchtime together. I was about to have a look at today's special when I suddenly heard the sound of a horn. So I looked up – and I saw this blue Volvo rushing past us and then we heard a screech of brakes. It was definitely driving way too fast! And then I noticed this red Mercedes, coming from the little cul-de-sac next to the café, trying to turn left into the main street. But its driver didn't see the Volvo coming because there was this big lorry blocking the view to the right. For quite some time the lorry driver had been unloading a huge delivery for the supermarket that is located next to the café. In addition to that, the sun has been shining brightly today, so it must have dazzled the driver. When the Mercedes driver moved forward to get a better view, it was already too late. The Volvo crashed into it.

The police officer:

3 Reported speech with modals – That's what I was told →G45

Put the following sentences into reported speech. Be careful not to change the meaning of the sentence.

1. Guide: You need not take off your shoes before walking through the castle. Large slippers to wear over your shoes will be provided.

2. Teacher: You must see the headmaster if you want to be granted a week off school.

3. Soccer coach: You must not let the other team intimidate you just because they're first in the local league.

4. Mother: You needn't help me in the kitchen today. I can do it alone.

5. Doctor: You should stop smoking at once, but as far as your lungs are concerned, it might be too late. You should not have started smoking in the first place. But you may know that already.

6. Teacher: You must read Shakespeare's plays. This way you'll get a deep insight into the human mind.

7. Police officer: You must not drive faster than 30 mph in this street.

4 Reporting commands, requests etc. – Correction, please! →G47

Each of the sentences below has been put into reported speech in two ways.
Have any mistakes been made in doing so? Correct them and write down (in German) what the mistakes were.

1. Father: I'll pick you up at the station at eight o'clock, Doreen.

a) Doreen's father promised he would pick her up at the station at eight o'clock.
b) Doreen's father offered Doreen to pick her up at the station at eight.

a) ______________________________

____

b) ______________________________

____

2. Teacher: Stop writing now, pupils, and pass your papers to the front.

a) The teacher ordered to stop writing and to pass the papers to the front.
b) The teacher wanted that the pupils stop writing and pass the papers to the front.

a) ______________________________

____

b) ______________________________

____

3. Doctor: You should take a hot bath and get some rest.

a) The doctor suggested taking a hot bath and to get some rest.
b) The doctor advised the patient that he took a hot bath and got some rest.

a) ______________________________

____

b) ______________________________

____

4. Police officer (to bank robber): Don't move!

a) The police officer warned the bank robber not to move.
b) The police officer insisted the bank robber not to move.

a) ______________________________

____

b) ______________________________

____

____

5. Security guard: You mustn't go into the cordoned off area.

a) The security guard ordered to not go into the cordoned off area.
b) The security guard instructed us not to go into the cordoned off area.

a) ______________________________

____

b) ______________________________

____

5 Reporting questions – An interview with an environmentalist (I) →G48

Below is an interview with Sue Morgan, a twenty-year-old student from Los Angeles. Sue is an environmentalist, trying to make a positive difference to the environment by keeping her carbon footprint as small as possible.

In your exercise book, write down the reported versions of the questions the interviewer asks Sue during the interview. (In exercise 6 that follows, you will be asked to write reported answers to these questions.)

Interview

1 **INTERVIEWER:** Sue, you're just 20, but you've had a long involvement with environmentalism. It started when you were a kid. What made you become active in environmentalism?

SUE: It was one specific thing. When I was in 4th grade, we celebrated Earth Day in elementary school for the first time, and we learned about the horrible things we humans do to the planet we live on every day. So I thought: Let's do something about it!

2 **INTERVIEWER:** So what did you do? Is there anything a 4th-grader can do to help save the Earth?

SUE: Oh yes, there is! First, I started riding my bike to school instead of having my mom drive me there. When we went shopping together, I started leaving the packaging in the supermarket. My mom didn't like it at first, because she thought she needed the instructions on it, but soon she was infected, too, and even started recycling herself!

3 **INTERVIEWER:** What about your friends? Did they think you were mad?

SUE: Not at all! They thought it was cool. They soon did the things I was doing, and the ones who lived farther away from school and could hardly come by bike started using public transportation. And guess what? Even their parents changed their lifestyles to a certain extent. That's what I call the "butterfly effect".

4 **INTERVIEWER:** What is this "butterfly effect"?

SUE: It's a theory saying that the flap of a butterfly's wings in Brazil can set off a tornado in Texas. The butterfly makes a tiny bit of air move, which is then intensified in a chain reaction until a tornado is set off. In the context of environmentalism that means: If you start acting green at home, it may have an intensified effect in the world – especially if others think you are doing the right thing!

5 **INTERVIEWER:** When did you take the next step towards environmentalism – in high school?

SUE: The older I got, the more I understood what people were doing wrong environmentally. I realized that saving water was equally important to reducing one's carbon emissions. So I didn't leave the tap running while brushing my teeth, I took showers instead of baths, and in the future, I'm definitely not going to have a pool in my garden! In high school, my friends and I became even more active – we founded a green club, did lots of fund-raising at school and in the neighborhood to donate the money to environmental non-profit organizations such as the WWF.

6 **INTERVIEWER:** You left high school three years ago and have started studying geo-engineering. Tell us something about this subject.

SUE: Sure. Basically, it's the science of engineering, but with the focus on how to use new technologies and inventions reasonably to help save the Earth. It starts with the research of alternative sources of energy and the development of biofuels, but it also means looking for ways of how to stop the destruction of the planet. Geo-engineering, for example, might one day find a way to repair the hole in the ozone layer and thus stop global warming. Wouldn't that be an achievement?

7 **INTERVIEWER:** It certainly would. But back to right now. Even if our readers don't have the money to change their lifestyle to a completely green one, what three low-cost things would you suggest to help the environment?

SUE: Do the easiest things first. One: Use energy-saving light bulbs and switch off energy-consuming devices as often as possible. Two: Sort and recycle your waste and reduce the packaging you take home. Three: Leave your car at home as often as possible and either use public transportation or cycle – this will even keep you fit! These are all cheap and easy things that can get you started with saving money right on the first day!

INTERVIEWER: Thank you so much for your advice, Sue, and for the interview. Good luck with your studies and good luck to all of us who now want to start living a greener lifestyle.

Aufbauniveau

6 Mixed exercise – An interview with an environmentalist (II) →G43–G49

Look again at the interview with Sue Morgan and the reported questions you wrote down in exercise 5. For each question, sum up Sue's answers in your exercise book by reporting more freely. Use wh-clauses, nouns or adjectives where appropriate.

Example:

Antwort zu 1: Sue outlined what first made her become envirionmentally active: a celebration of Earth Day when she was in elementary school. The things people did to the planet shocked her and she decided to take action.

Antwort zu 2: ______

7 Attention, please! →G50

The following signs can be found at airports. Rephrase the signs, using "that + present subjunctive" to make the order sound formal (if it is unclear who gave the order, use an impersonal it-construction such as "it is necessary that …").

Example:

The airport police advise that luggage not be left unattended.

8 Stone Cold →G51

The following text is an extract from Robert Swindells' novel *Stone Cold*.
A former army sergeant who calls himself Shelter "recruits" homeless teenagers in London for a very special army of his own. The extract is written from Shelter's perspective. He contemplates the preparations he has made to make his victims trust him more easily and follow him into his house …

Put Shelter's thoughts (written from the 1st person point of view) into free indirect speech.

It is 19.00 hours and this has been a most satisfactory day. Most satisfactory. The secret of victory in any campaign is planning and preparation. My planning has been meticulous*, and my preparations are now complete.
I have acquired a cat. This was my finishing touch. I can't abide* the […] hair-scattering beasts myself, but you have to admit there's something reassuring about a home with a cat in it. A cat speaks of warmth, comfort, placid domesticity*.
A man who keeps a cat can't possibly mean anybody harm, can he?
I've christened* it Sappho. A brilliant touch this, suggesting as it does a degree of scholarship* in the creature's owner.
I don't even know whether the bloody thing's male or female and I don't care – the point is that a feller* with a cat called Sappho is going to project a certain sort of image. Kindly and a bit academic.
He might be expected to have a vague conscience about sleeping snug* and warm while others live rough. He'll be a bumbler*, but he might be stirred now and then to actually do something about this – to offer grub* and a bed for the night to some poor unfortunate soul, no strings attached*.
So it's Shelter and Sappho. Could be a series on the telly, couldn't it? Shelter and Sappho, otherwise known as The Invincibles. All is ready. Recruiting can now commence.

Robert Swindells, *Stone Cold*, 1993

It was 19.00 hours and this had been a most satisfactory day. Most satisfactory.

*__meticulous__ – sorgfältig; __abide__ – ausstehen; __domesticity__ – ruhige Häuslichkeit; __christen__ – taufen; __scholarship__ – Gelehrsamkeit; __feller__ – *fellow*; __snug__ – behaglich; __bumbler__ – Tollpatsch; __grub__ – *food*; __no strings attached__ – ohne Gegenleistung

7 Relativsätze

Grundniveau

1 Relative clauses – Defining and non-defining →G53, G54

When you give explanations or background information, it is often advisable to use defining and non-defining relative clauses.

Example:

precious metal — gold — mainly used for jewellery

a) Defining: Gold is a precious metal which is mainly used for jewellery.
Defining: The precious metal which is mainly used for jewellery is gold.

b) Non-defining: Gold, which is a precious metal, is mainly used for jewellery.
Non-defining: Gold, which is mainly used for jewellery, is a precious metal.

Use the following phrases to give explanations or background information. In each case use one defining and one non-defining clause. You may have to add a word or use the passive. Write in your exercise book.

1. modern British playwright — Harold Pinter — awarded the Nobel Prize for Literature in 2005
2. extreme sport — kite surfing — combines windsurfing and paragliding
3. nocturnal New Zealand bird — kiwi — in danger of becoming extinct
4. nautical instrument — sextant — seamen use it to calculate the position of their ship
5. English composer — Edward Elgar — wrote the music to "Land of Hope and Glory"
6. undercover agents on planes — sky marshals — task is to prevent hijacking
7. building in Philadelphia — Independence Hall — US Declaration of Independence proclaimed
8. government official — ombudsman — job is to deal with complaints against institutions
9. medical specialist — dermatologist — patients with skin problems consult him

2 Present and past participle replacing a relative clause →G53

a) *Change the sentence construction, using **who, which** or **whose** in relative clauses. Be careful with the tenses!*

1. The man crossing the road right now is our new neighbour.
2. Motorists driving under the influence of drugs or alcohol are likely to cause accidents.
3. Already sitting in his car, Freddy waved us goodbye.
4. People with children suffering from leukaemia have a lot of worry and fear.
5. There has just been a terror warning for all planes flying to Syria this time tomorrow.
6. Completed in 1937, the Golden Gate Bridge has become a famous landmark of San Francisco.
7. Anyone found guilty of drug possession in Singapore faces the death penalty.
8. He is one of the top international players taking part in the World Cup next month.

b) *Replace the relative clauses with an appropriate participle.*

1. The Globe Theatre, which was built as a faithful reconstruction of an Elizabethan theatre, is popular with visitors to London.
2. Rita, who wondered why her boyfriend had not arrived yet, called him on his mobile.
3. The supervisor carefully watched the students who were taking the exam.
4. Students who were caught cheating did not receive a pass grade.
5. The demonstrators who wanted to protest violently refused to negotiate with the police.
6. Immigrants who have been living in that country for over ten years will now be given automatic citizenship.
7. Passengers who are travelling first class will be served dinner immediately.
8. People whose dogs are considered dangerous have to keep them under control at all times.

3 Joining sentences with relative clauses →G52, G53

Combine the following sentences with the help of relative pronouns. Put in commas where necessary.

1. Mrs Taylor is talking to a customer. He wants to buy a pushchair.
2. I am looking after some cats. They are extremely lively.
3. The shop was burgled last night. Mrs Wilson works in this shop.
4. "Lord of the Flies" is the story of a group of public school boys. Their plane has crashed on an uninhabited island.
5. The rock fell on a group of mountaineers. Three of them were killed.
6. Miss Purdy flew to Paris. She had always wanted to visit it.
7. The report has dismayed the nation. According to it, 30 per cent of the population is living below the poverty line.
8. Fergus has moved to Glasgow. We haven't heard from him for months.
9. The Isle of Skye is always worth a visit. Its scenery is breathtaking.

4 Using relative clauses to improve texts →G52, G53, G55

With the help of relative pronouns, make one sentence from the information given. Put in commas where necessary.

1. We had a ride on the London Eye. This enabled us to enjoy the magnificent view. We had been told a lot about this view.
2. Mr Gaskell came to the ball in fancy dress. This amused the other guests. All of the other guests were wearing evening dress.

3. In the meeting Mr Brown was sitting on a chair. It suddenly collapsed. This made everybody laugh.

___

___

4. "Romeo and Juliet" is a play by Shakespeare. It depicts the fate of two lovers. Their families hate each other.

___

___

5. In 1967 Francis Chichester sailed round the world single-handed. This had never been done before. He was later knighted by Queen Elizabeth II.

___

___

6. A lorry skidded on the road. The road was flooded after a sudden downpour. Then it crashed into a bus. Seven of the nineteen passengers on the bus were injured.

___

___

___

7. Going to Rome I missed the plane. I had been booked on this plane. [and] I had to take the next flight. This was not a direct one.

___

___

8. A group of girls were skinny-dipping in the lake. The village boys thoroughly enjoyed this. They were watching them.

___

___

5 Clauses with *which* and *what* →G55, G56

*Fill the gaps in the following sentences by using either **which** or **what**. Put in commas where necessary.*

Example: He did what ___ he could , which ___ was unfortunately not enough.

1. One cannot be held responsible for ___ one thinks.
2. She laughed at his marriage proposal ___ really hurt his feelings.
3. Sally didn't believe ___ they told her ___ annoyed them very much.
4. The visitors were not surprised at ___ they saw because the guide had told them ___ to expect.
5. Derek bought himself a new laptop ___ was exactly ___ I had told him to do.
6. ___ he expected me to do was impossible ___ I bluntly told him.
7. Global warming is causing climate change, because of ___ new policies on energy are needed ___ most governments are now adopting.
8. His party suffered considerable losses and ___ came as a particular shock to him, he was not re-elected.
9. His party suffered considerable losses and he was not re-elected ___ came as a particular shock to him.

6 Defining, non-defining and sentence relative clauses →G53, G55, G57

Compare the following sentence pairs. What is the difference in meaning between the two sentences? Explain in German.

Example:
a) My sister, who got married last week, lives in Edinburgh.
b) My sister who got married last week lives in Edinburgh.

a) Meine einzige Schwester wohnt in Edinburgh und sie heiratete.

b) Von meinen Schwestern heiratete diejenige, die in Edinburgh wohnt.

1. a) The hikers, who knew about the rockfall, took a different route.
   b) The hikers who knew about the rockfall took a different route.

   a) ______

   b) ______

2. a) Ben gave me a present, which I had not expected.
   b) Ben gave me a present which I had not expected.

   a) ______

   b) ______

3. a) Last night Alex went to a concert which was very unusual.
   b) Last night Alex went to a concert, which was very unusual.

   a) ______

   b) ______

4. a) Before the concert started, the conductor made an announcement which annoyed the audience.
   b) Before the concert started, the conductor made an announcement, which annoyed the audience.

   a) ______

   b) ______

5. a) My grandfather who is an engineer is going to retire next year.
   b) My grandfather, who is an engineer, is going to retire next year.

   a) ______

   b) ______

6. a) Liza turned up at the party in a dress which gave the other guests something to talk about.
   b) Liza turned up at the party in a dress, which gave the other guests something to talk about.

   a) ______

   b) ______

7. a) On summer evenings, when the air was warm, they used to have dinner out on the patio.
   b) On summer evenings when the air was warm they used to have dinner out on the patio.

   a) ______

   b) ______

8. a) Many people prefer to live in cities, where there is a wide range of cultural activities.
   b) Many people prefer to live in cities where there is a wide range of cultural activities.

   a) ______

   b) ______

7 Defining and non-defining relative clauses →G52–G57

Insert relative pronouns or relative adverbs – in brackets if they are dispensable (contact clauses). Put in commas where necessary.

James and Amy

James was in a rut. He was almost forty and ____________ was worse, still single. He decided to take a late autumn break in Cornwall ____________ he had often been as a child. During the week ____________ he spent there he met his future wife. Amy was also nearly forty. The man of ____________ she dreamt had never turned up so when she saw James in an empty café, she asked if the other chair at the table was taken. James was overwhelmed. She was the first woman ____________ had taken any interest in him. After a few days, during ____________ they went for long walks, he couldn't think of any good reason ____________ he shouldn't marry her. They were living in an age ____________ a man had to ask a woman's father for her hand in marriage so Amy arranged a meeting with her parents ____________ went well. Most people prefer to get married in spring ____________ the weather is better, but neither James nor Amy could wait. She suggested a church ____________ vicar was a friend of her father's and they got married a week before Christmas. His parents didn't come to the wedding ____________ annoyed him considerably, but otherwise it was a great success. They had a reception in a hotel on the cliffs, after ____________ the newly married couple left for London. ____________ James was most nervous about was how Amy would like living in London. He needn't have worried; the woman ____________ had lived all her life in the country took to life in the big city at once. Years later they returned to Cornwall, but the church ____________ they were married had been demolished.

8 Adding information with the help of relative clauses →G52–G55, G57

Use relative clauses to improve the text on Thomas Alva Edison by inserting in the right places the additional information from the blue list. (Mark these places in the original text and rewrite it with the inserted relative clauses in your exercise book.)

Thomas Alva Edison

Thomas Alva Edison was born in Milan on February 11, 1847.
He is famous for having created and patented numerous devices. Furthermore, he is widely regarded as having established the world's first research laboratory. The aim of this laboratory was to ensure ongoing innovation in a wide range of technological fields. Moreover, his commercial acumen enabled him and his staff to generate maximum profits thanks to mass production and the acquisition of patent rights.
As Edison was considered stupid and intractable by his teacher, he left school after only three months. From then on he was taught at home by his mother.
During his early years he avidly read R.G. Parker's *School of Natural Philosophy* and Thomas Paine's The *Age of Reason*. Later he enrolled in a chemistry course at The Cooper Union.
A station agent named MacKenzie gave him training as a telegraph operator. Therefore it is hardly surprising that some of his first inventions were connected to telegraphy.
Edison was married twice, first to Mary Stilwell and then to Mina Miller. Altogether he had six children.
The legendary inventor Edison died in New Jersey on October 18, 1931, at the ripe old age of 84.

Additional information

1. Thomas Alva Edison was an American inventor and businessman.
2. Milan is a small town in Ohio.
3. Among the devices he created were the phonograph, the motion picture camera and a practical electric light bulb.
4. Edison's laboratory was situated in Menlo Park.
5. Menlo Park is a township in New Jersey. It was renamed "Edison" in 1954.
6. In this laboratory research and development were carried out under Edison's strict guidance.
7. Mass production and patent rights were the key to his phenomenal success.
8. Edison's parents had six other children.
9. He remained eternally grateful to his mother for teaching him.
10. The School of Natural Philosophy is a sort of science primer.
11. The primer describes experiments.
12. He acquired much of his knowledge from these two books.
13. The Cooper Union is a private full-scholarship college.
14. It is located in New York.
15. MacKenzie's three-year-old son had been rescued by Edison from a runaway train.
16. To a certain extent this training launched him on his career.
17. One of these first inventions was a stock ticker.
18. Edison wed Mary when she was only 16.
19. Two of his children later also became inventors and another of his children was elected Governor of New Jersey.
20. His nation is rightly proud of Edison.

Aufbauniveau

9 Generalising relative pronouns →G58

Translate the following sentences into English, using generalising relative pronouns. Write in your exercise book.

1. Wer das Rad erfand, leistete zweifelsohne einen wichtigen Beitrag zum technologischen Fortschritt.
2. Du kannst mich anrufen, wann immer es dir passt.
3. In seiner neuen Stellung ist er für alles verantwortlich, was mit der Sicherheit am Arbeitsplatz zu tun hat.
4. Dies ist Ihre Auswahl an Aufsatzthemen. Wählen Sie dasjenige, das Sie am besten behandeln können.
5. Wohin Edmund Hillary auch blickte, sah er nichts als die eisigen Bergspitzen des Himalaja.
6. Die Partei wird denjenigen zum Kandidaten ernennen*, den sie für dieses Amt für am besten geeignet hält.
7. Flüchtlinge müssen fair behandelt werden, gleich aus welchem Land sie kommen.
8. Von allen Mitarbeitern wird erwartet, dass sie die Regeln befolgen, ganz gleich, wie sie persönlich dazu stehen*.
9. Die meisten Kinder, die zweisprachig aufgewachsen sind, können fließend kommunizieren, gleich welche Sprache sie benutzen.

10 Relative clauses with *where-* →G59

Give a suitable substitute for the relative adverb on the line under each sentence. Then translate the sentence into appropriate German in your exercise book.

1. The plight wherein the castaways found themselves seemed desperate.

____

____

2. I know whereof I speak.

____

3. They inspected the safe wherein all the treaties and documents were preserved.

____

____

4. The Lisbon Treaty of 2009 contains an arrangement whereby the EU presidency rotates among all member states every half year.

____

5. As their applications for asylum had been turned down, the refugees were sent back whence they had fled.

____

6. The company introduced a new regulation whereby smoking was prohibited during working hours.

____

7. The manager announced the closing of the local branch, whereupon a tumult broke out among the employees.

____

8. The ideals whereon the nation was based were liberty, equality and the rule of law.

____

*__ernennen__ – appoint; __zu etwas stehen__ – feel about sth

8 Bedingungen ausdrücken

Grundniveau

1 Conditional sentences – Basic patterns →G60

Complete the sentences with the appropriate form of the verb.

1. It's only human to put the blame on others.
If you ______________________ (blame) other people, you ______________________ (make) them responsible for a mistake.
2. Sam: Ian is a journalist. He writes 1,200 words a day and earns £500 a week. That's not enough to buy a house.
Michael: Well, if he ______________________ (want) to make more money, he ______________________ (have) to do more work. Unless he ______________________ (work) harder, he ______________________________ (be able) to buy a house.
3. We have been here too long. We should go home now. If we ______________________ (not go) home now, it ______________________ (be) midnight before we get back.
4. Charly: What is the difference between a wage and a salary?
Teacher: If you ______________________ (earn) a wage, your firm ______________________ (pay) you once a week; if payment ______________________ (be) monthly, you ______________________ (receive) a salary.
5. Gordon: This country spends too much money on useless things.
Geoff: You're absolutely right. If I ______________________ (be) Prime Minister, I ______________________ (spend) a lot more money on education.
6. John: I hate being alone.
Sarah: What ____________________________ (you, do) if you __________________ (be) on a desert island?
7. Gloria: Yesterday we went to Manchester by car. It took us more than five hours.
Barbara: If you ______________________ (go) by train instead of by car, you __________________________ (arrive) in less than half the time.
8. Bill: I am always seasick when I cross the English Channel.
Harry: If you ____________________________________ (always, get) seasick, why on earth ____ (you, not take) the Eurostar?

2 Conditional sentences – Real and unreal conditions →G61–G63

Translate the German into English using the correct forms of the verbs.

1. Wenn man Leute darum bittet, helfen sie einem meistens bereitwillig*. Hättest du das im Hinterkopf gehabt*, hättest du es im Urlaub einfacher gehabt.

2. Wenn es den ganzen Tag regnete, blieben seine Großeltern zu Hause und lasen. Wenn Tom das gewusst hätte, hätte er seinen Kindle mitgenommen, als er sie besuchte.

3. Wenn du Milch nicht im Kühlschrank aufbewahrst, wird sie schnell schlecht*. Wenn du sie also nicht zurückstellst, wirst du keine Milch für deine Cornflakes haben.

4. Mein Vater fuhr oft nach England. Wenn er nach London ging, besuchte er immer das Globe Theater. Wenn ich mit ihm mitgegangen wäre, hätte ich die Zeit lieber* in den interessanten historischen Pubs verbracht!

5. Wenn du London besuchen willst, empfehle ich dir im Internet zu schauen. Wenn du dich richtig vorbereiten würdest, hättest du mehr von* deinem Trip.

6. Sollte man Urlaub nur im eigenen Land machen? Wenn man mich gefragt hätte, hätte ich die Antwort nicht gewusst. Aber wenn man den CO_2-Ausstoß* ernst nimmt, muss man irgendwo anfangen.

7. Hätte meine Mutter gewusst, dass Spanien so teuer ist, hätten wir bestimmt einen Urlaub in einem preiswerteren Land wie der Türkei gebucht. Auf der anderen Seite ist es schwer, sie umzustimmen, wenn sie etwas beschlossen hat.

8. Wenn das Wetter im Winter schlecht ist, träumen die meisten Menschen von einem Urlaub an einem sonnigen Strand. Würdest du in der Karibik* wohnen, müsstest du nicht träumen. Du hättest aber auch kein schlechtes Wetter im Winter.

* **bereitwillig helfen** – be willing to help; **etwas im Hintergrund halten** – keep in mind; **schlecht werden** – go off; **lieber** – rather; **mehr von etwas haben** – get more out of sth.; **CO_2-Ausstoß** – CO_2 emissions; **die Karibik** – the Caribbean

3 Mixed exercise – The director →G61–G63

A French film won a lot of awards at the Oscars in Hollywood. Read the director's thank you speech, mark the mistakes in the use of conditionals and correct them in the space between the lines.

Thank you for this wonderful prize. But I want to thank a lot of other people, too.

I had never had the idea for the film if my wife hadn't told me an interesting story.

Thank you, my darling!

I would also like to thank the crew at the studio. Nothing was too much trouble.

If I would need to work at night, they would sleep at the studio. I didn't know that at the time.

If I had known that, I had not shouted at them so much!

And thank you to my distributor in America for his faith in the film.

He said, "As soon as news of the film will get to America, people will want to see it."

He was right and then it was like a snowball.

You see, if people will like a film, they tell their friends about it.

So, thanks to everybody who told their friends about my film. I'm sorry for my bad English.

If I hadn't been so busy in the last few months, I had could prepare a better speech for this evening.

But now it's party time.

I said to everybody involved in the film, "If we win an award, I throw the biggest party you've ever seen."

4 Unreal present and past conditions →G62, G63

Complete the sentences, using the correct conditionals as appropriate.

1. If Oliver had had time, he ______________________ (shave) before he went to the disco. Maybe then he ______________________ (dance) more often. And if he______________________ (take) his cigarette out of his mouth, his girlfriend______________________ (give) him a kiss.
2. If Dick ate less, he ______________________ (not have to) go on a diet. And if he ______________________ (brush) his teeth more regularly, he ______________________ (still have) more teeth in his mouth.
3. You know, my parents are to blame for my accident. If they ______________________ (lend) me their sat-nav*, I ______________________ (not have to) look at the map and I ______________________ (see) the red light. The accident at the crossroads ______________________ (avoid).
4. Most English people hate sauerkraut and love German beer. If we ______________________ (know) you were different, we ______________________ (offer) you sauerkraut and you ______________________ (not give) beer to drink. You ______________________ (even, enjoy) German white wine, which is the best white wine in the world.
5. Neil moved into his new flat last week. Now his landlord says he needs the flat for his daughter. If Neil had known that before he moved in, he ______________________ (drop) the whole idea. He ______________________ (realise) that he ______________________ (be) better off if he ______________________ (stay) in his old place.

* sat-nav – Navi

6. Don't be so rude about English food! If you ______________ (try) spotted dick*, shepherd's pie and fish and chips, you ______________ (find) that you like them. They ______________ (even become) part of your normal diet back in Germany.
7. If the weather in California ______________ (be) so bad, I ______________ (go) surfing every day. Sadly, I never did.
8. If politicians ______________ (admit) their mistakes occasionally, voters ______________ (believe) them more. At least it ______________ (improve) their reputations.

5 Mixed exercise – Error spotting →G61–G63

Are there any errors in these sentences? If there are, mark them and correct them on the right.

1. If I am tired and can't sleep, I start reading a book and immediately fall asleep. ______________
2. Maria is worried about her exam. If she made an effort, she passed it. ______________
3. When he is from Mexico, he is not likely to speak English and more likely to speak Spanish. ______________
4. If she would wear smarter clothes, she had more success at interviews. ______________
5. In Germany you can't go hunting unless you don't have a hunting license. ______________
6. If you would like to speak to me about the project, please send me an e-mail or call my mobile number. ______________
7. Who would you bring if I will invite you to my brithday party next Saturday? ______________
8. She might have qualified for the Olympics if only she trained more regularly. ______________
9. We hadn't missed the train, if we would have got up as planned. ______________
10. If they had a long trip ahead of them, they got up as early as they could. ______________

* **spotted dick** – gedämpfter Pudding

6 German "wenn" →G64

Translate these sentences into English.

1. Wir haben es bewiesen. Wenn schlechte Zeiten kommen, ist diese Partei immer für Sie da.

2. Und wir versprechen: Wenn schlechte Zeiten kommen, ist diese Partei immer für Sie da.

3. Das Ende der Finanzkrise ist in Sicht, und wenn die Konjunktur anzieht, wird die Arbeitslosigkeit sinken.

4. Alle hoffen, dass die Maßnahmen greifen werden, weil die Arbeitslosigkeit sinken wird, wenn die Konjunktur anzieht.

5. Wenn sie nach England gingen, würden sie all ihre Freunde besuchen.

6. Wenn sie nach England gingen, haben sie immer all ihre Freunde besucht.

7. Es tut mir leid, aber wir müssen warten. Wir essen erst, wenn George kommt.

8. Antonio hilft immer, wenn ich einen deutschen Text ins Italienische übertragen muss.

9. Wenn er das wirklich gesagt hat, wusste er nicht, dass es dir wehtun würde.

10. Als er das gesagt hat, wusste er nicht, dass du im Zimmer warst.

11. Wenn du ihn um Hilfe bitten würdest, würde er sofort vorbeikommen.

12. Wenn du ihn um Hilfe gebeten hast, kam er immer sofort vorbei.

Aufbauniveau

7 Conditional sentences – Advanced patterns →G65

Complete the sentences using the tense given. You are free to write whatever you like, only it must make sense!

1. If she's waiting at the station, … ______________________________ (will future)
2. If they've been practising every day, … ______________________________ (simple present)
3. If the ferry is late, … ______________________________ (simple past)
4. If the winter lasts until April, … ______________________________ (imperative/modal verb)
5. If you're expecting me to apologise, … ______________________________ (imperative/modal verb)
6. If they're flying to Greece on holiday, … ______________________________ (present perfect)
7. If the exams had gone badly, … ______________________________ (simple past)
8. If they met by chance, … ______________________________ (conditional I)
9. If his work was getting on his nerves, … ______________________________ (simple past)
10. If the planning had been better, … ______________________________ (conditional I)
11. If you practised more, … ______________________________ (conditional II/conditional perfect)

8 Mixed exercise – Conditions with *If + will/would* and *If + were* →G66, G67

Using the information in the first sentence, complete the second sentence. In each case use an appropriate way of expressing a condition.

1. You always do your homework at the last minute.
   ______________________________,
   you shouldn't be surprised that you get half of it wrong!
2. It's two o'clock in the morning!
   I'd like to hear the end of your story ______________________________
3. Please give us a quick reply.
   We'd be really grateful ______________________________

4. He refuses to listen to any criticism.

____

it's not surprising his work keeps getting worse.

5. There's a car parked in front of our house.

We'd be able to unload the van more easily ____

____

6. I can't stand the way she always has the last word.

____

it's no wonder no one wants to discuss anything with her.

7. I'm busy right now but I'll be free in five minutes.

____,

I'll be able to deal with your problem without any interruptions.

8. Might I ask you to speak to the manager?

It would really be a great help to me ____

____

9. Charles's wife is so impossibly bossy.

We'd have a wonderful weekend in the country ____

____

9 Conditions without an *if*-clause →G68

Using the information in the first sentence, complete the second sentence. In each case express a condition without an if-clause.

1. Thank you so much for your advice.

____

I would have made a big mistake.

2. You must work hard for your exams.

You'll pass your exams ____

3. It's a good thing he was given a second chance.

____,

he'd have spent all his life in prison.

4. He should think about his argument with Lisa again.

____,

he'd realise he was very unfair to her.

5. We must make sure we have enough time for the art gallery.

Let's forget about the walk in the park. ____

____

9 Adverbialsätze und infinite Konstruktionen

Grundniveau

1 Participle and gerund constructions instead of adverbial clauses →G70

Link the following sentences by using gerund or participle constructions.

Example:
He was tired. He went to bed.
Being tired he went to bed.

Sometimes you must use the words in brackets, too. ***(instead of; though; by)***
Be careful: One of the sentence pairs cannot be linked by a participle construction. Say why.

1. He came home late. He saw his house had been broken into.
______
2. Don't go by car. You should take the bus to the city centre.
______
3. Take the bus! Then you won't have to look for a place to park.
______
4. He arrived at the station. The train had already left.
______
5. She didn't speak any French at all. She managed to get along in Paris quite well.
______
6. You won't have any problems with this exercise. You are a clever student!
______
7. The car passed by at great speed. This made it impossible to recognise the driver.
______
8. They weren't informed about the change of plan. They missed the outing to the lake.
______
9. She watched *Rebecca* on television. After that she decided to read the book.
______
10. Energy drinks are often consumed in large quantities. This can cause health problems.
______

2 Shortening relative clauses →G71

Shorten these sentences with participle constructions. Decide whether present or past participles are required.

Example:
I like this poster which was given to me by a friend.
I like this poster given to me by a friend.

1. In this fortress a pirate who was known by the name of Black Beard was hanged.
2. The tree which stood close to the main entrance had to be cut down.
3. The man who is being questioned by the police was arrested yesterday.
4. The task which closes the exam will be a translation.
5. The E-type Jaguar, which was built in the 1960s, is considered to be a classic British sports car.
6. The new statistics, which were very detailed, presented a realistic basis for future planning.
7. The man who doesn't wish to have his photo in the paper has a profile on the social networks.
8. The houses on the left side of the street, which were hardly damaged in the 2010 earthquake, burned down last year.

3 Participle constructions →G70, G71

Improve the following text by using participle constructions whenever possible. Write in your exercise book.

When you watch a cricket match for the first time, you may find it puzzling, so I'll explain the rules. Here come the players onto the field. They are wearing white shirts. The man who throws the ball is the bowler. He throws it at three sticks which are called the wicket. The man over there who is standing in front of the wicket is the batsman. After the bowler has thrown his ball, the batsman tries to hit it with his bat. When he has hit the ball, the batsman runs from his wicket to the other wicket and back as often as possible. Around the wickets there are eleven players who belong to the opposing team. When the ball flies through the air, they try to catch it.
The ball is sometimes hard to see because it is so small. A batsman who is still running between the two wickets when the other team hits the wicket with the ball is out.
The team that has scored more runs before their batsmen are all out has won the match. Although matches last for hours, they are followed closely by the spectators. Many Englishmen, who have often played a lot of cricket at school, get excited when they watch a cricket match.

4 Infinitive constructions – Contrast to constructions in German →G73

Translate these words of a well-intentioned German father into English, using infinitive constructions.

Example:
Es ist gut, wenn man weiß, wo man nachschauen muss.
It is good to know where to look things up.

1. Du fragst dich*, ob du die Schule verlassen oder bleiben und einen Abschluss machen* sollst.
____
2. Als dein Vater wird von mir erwartet, dass ich dir beistehe*.
____
3. Ich möchte, dass du später einmal einen guten Job bekommst.
____
4. Deshalb ist es wichtig für dich, dass du eine gute Ausbildung* erhältst.
____
5. Aber ich will auch, dass du glücklich bist.
____
6. Es ist Zeit, dass du herausfindest, wo deine Begabungen* liegen.
____
7. Dann wirst du wissen, was du tun musst.
____

5 Gerund or infinitive constructions →G72, G73

Decide whether gerunds or infinitives are necessary. You may need an appropriate preposition in connection with a gerund.

Our family is tired _______________ (live) in the city. My father hates _______________ (go) to work with all that noise , traffic and smog in the morning and he doesn't want _______________ (hear) police cars with their sirens _______________ (pass by) all the time.
Instead _______________ (get) stuck in traffic jams he would like _______________ (travel) by train. So we are really looking forward _______________ (move) to the country. We hope _______________ (find) a nice house with a garden where we will enjoy _______________ (have) breakfast in clean air every morning. Of course there is the danger _______________ (get) bored at the weekends with no cinemas or theatres around, but it will be worth _______________ (try).

*sich fragen – wonder; **einen Abschluss machen** – get a certificate; **jdm beistehen** – stand by sb; **Ausbildung** – education; **Begabungen** – talents

6 Infinitive constructions →G73

Rewrite these texts in your exercise book. Use as many infinitive constructions as possible.

Jason Brothers Ltd sold to Chinese investor

Jason Brothers Ltd had an idea for a new product which would improve sales and went to their bank. They did this because they wanted to borrow money. They borrowed over five million pounds, which the bank arranged. A year later the bank thought they would pay back their debt as expected but they couldn't. So they extended the loan, which the bank allowed. Firms renegotiate loans – this is quite normal – but no one from Jason Brothers called the bank. The firm had huge debts. So, under pressure from the bank, Jason Brothers looked for an investor They tried to find an investor in Europe but it was too difficult. Then the Chinese came …

American astronauts were the first who landed on the moon. Of course they had a lot of equipment that helped them. Of the three astronauts who took off from Earth only two landed on the moon because the room in the lunar module meant only two people could live in it. Since their training on earth had been thorough, they knew exactly when they should fire their rockets and where they could land. They had a strict plan because there were so many things they had to do. They gathered lunar rock so they often moved away from the lunar module. They had to be back in the lunar module at a certain time. This was very important.

7 Expressing the German "lassen" →G74

a) *Decide which sense of "lassen" is being used in each case and translate the sentences.*

1. Mein Vater lässt mich jeden Samstag unser Auto waschen. Ich hasse das!

   ____

2. Glücklicherweise lässt sich das Auto schnell waschen.

   ____

3. Meine Mutter lässt ihr Auto in der Waschanlage waschen.

   ____

4. Mein Bruder lässt niemanden sein Auto anfassen!

   ____

b) *Decide which is the correct translation of the German sentences.*

1. Ich werde ihn für seine Verbrechen bezahlen lassen.
   - ☐ a) I'll let him pay for his crimes.
   - ☐ b) I'll have him pay for his crimes.
   - ☐ c) I'll make him pay for his crimes.

2. Wir lassen auch Gäste an unseren Debatten teilnehmen.
   - ☐ a) We also have guests participate in our debates.
   - ☐ b) We also make guests participate in our debates.
   - ☐ c) We also let guests participate in our debates.

3. Er hat seinen Computer reparieren lassen.
   - ☐ a) He has repaired his computer.
   - ☐ b) He has had his computer repaired.
   - ☐ c) He has let his computer be repaired.

4. Die Rebellen ließen ihn sogar in Winter draußen schlafen.
   - ☐ a) The rebels even allowed him to sleep outside in winter.
   - ☐ b) The rebels even forced him to sleep outside in winter.
   - ☐ c) The rebels even persuaded him to sleep outside in winter.

8 Gerund or infinitive constructions after certain verbs →G75

Complete the following sentence pairs, using the verb in brackets. For one use a gerund construction and for the other an infinitive construction. Then note in German the difference in meaning.

1. a) I can't remember ______________________ (invite) so many people to my party.
b) Fortunately I remembered ______________________ (buy) enough to drink.

____

____

2. a) I regret ______________________ (tell) you that the flight is already fully booked.
b) I regret ______________________ (advise) you to fly at the weekend.

____

____

3. a) Don't forget ______________________ (take) a dictionary with you for your exam.
b) You will never forget ______________________ (sit) your exam without a dictionary.

____

____

4. a) I'm going to try ______________________ (get) a job with an airline next week.
b) I will try ______________________ (use) the internet when I look for my next job.

____

____

5. a) Tact sometimes means ______________________ (not say) exactly what you think.
b) This time she really means ______________________ (not stop) until she's reached her goal.

____

____

6. a) Aren't you going to stop ______________________ (look at) this wonderful view?
b) Aren't you going to stop ______________________ (hold) us up all the time?

____

____

7. a) It was so boring. He went on ______________________ (talk) about his operation the whole evening.
b) Then he went on ______________________ (describe) in detail his stay in hospital.

____

____

8. a) The number of students will continue ______________________ (increase) until the end of the decade.
b) The government announced it will continue ______________________ (increase) investment in alternative energy.

____

____

____

9 Infinite constructions – Translating into German →G70, G71, G73

Translate the following short texts containing infinite constructions into idiomatic German. Pay careful attention to the relationship between finite and non-finite clauses.

1. **Having** different functions, the two news-reporting media, newspapers and TV, continue to exist side by side.
   A newspaper is expected to express a clear viewpoint, nearly each one **representing** a political position, though not in the sense of party politics.
   On the other hand, television **is expected to** give unbiased news reports, not **parading** an editorial position of its own, always **presenting** both sides of the argument, **balancing** the views of different political parties, the reporters **instructed** by their employers to analyse the situation carefully and objectively.

2. **Making** high quality university education widely available, we enable talented students to develop and benefit from their abilities. Though **providing** an **opportunity for young people to** move up in society, not all pupils can take advantage of the system – some **not having** the academic background **needed to be accepted** for higher education and others **prepared** for the challenges ahead but not **possessing** the confidence to be **the first in their family to** go to university.

Aufbauniveau

10 Participle and gerund constructions with their own subject →G76

Link the following sentences using participle and gerund constructions. You need "with" in some cases!

Example:
Our choir sings the Halleluja chorus. I love it.
I love our choir singing the Halleluja chorus.

1. My mom kisses me goodbye in front of my friends. I hate it!

____

____

2. The banks pay huge bonuses to their managers despite the crisis. The government dislikes that.

____

____

3. The comedy was such a success. The tour had to be extended.

____

4. John won the school tennis trophy. Everyone is very surprised at that!

____

5. The car crashed into the shop window. We saw it.

____

6. The rain was pouring down so heavily. The open-air festival had to be cancelled.

____

7. The bike was speeding down the road. I couldn't hear it.

____

8. The runners finally reached the home stretch. Most spectators cheered whenever one passed.

____

9. Becky struggled to keep up with the rest of the hiking group. They didn't notice it.

____

10. He flirts with her at every opportunity. I just can't stand that.

____

Focus B

1 A Prime Minister under presssure →K7–K9

Find the errors in the text and correct them in the spaces between the lines.

Melanie Crawford is one of the nation's best-known broadcasters, who's parents also worked in television.

She has her own current affairs programme on nationwide television and is known for her aggressive interviewing style. Every week she interviewed politicians on her programme but which she really wanted was to interview the Prime Minister. Her reputation were certainly enhanced if she would have the chance to talk to him on her programme. Her programme director suggested her to send him an invitation to appear on the next programme. All what she needed to do was send a letter to Downing Street.

After having thought about it for a few days, the Prime Minister wrote back that he was looking forward to talk to her about government policy.

The interview started amicably enough, what disappointed most viewers who wanted that the Prime Minister got angry and made a scene.

Melanie Crawford made the Prime Minister talk about his government's first year in office, without to comment on any failures. Then to liven up the interview Melanie Crawford asked him several difficult questions about government policy.

The Prime Minister remained cool. So she tried to ask him questions about his private finances.

Since not wanting to talk about personal matters, the Prime Minister tried changing the subject but she kept on ask the same question until the Prime Minister started shouting at her.

Afterwards she said, "If politicians won't answer questions, I'll ask them over and over again until they do." Viewers were unanimous in their judgement: If the Prime Minister were cleverer, he would have given some sort of vague answer. It was a programme which effect lasted a long time.

From that day the Prime Minister became known as the politician, who lost his temper on television. She became more popular than ever, although her programme director let her write an open letter to the Prime Minister in which she regretted to question him about private matters. In his reply he asked her if she'd like spending a week following his work in Parliament. She refused, saying there should always be a professional distance between journalists and politicians.

2 Queen Elizabeth II and her Diamond Jubilee →K5–K9

Rewrite the following text in your exercise book. You have to:

- *choose the correct modal(s)* **MO**
- *rephrase the sentence by creating an if-clause* **IF**
- *use a participle, gerund or an infinitive construction, adding a preposition if necessary* **CO**
- *put in the correct relative pronoun* **RP**
- *change direct speech into reported speech* **RS**

Why, people from the Continent ... **MO** wonder, are the English so infatuated* with their current monarch, Elizabeth II?
On the Sunday of her jubilee weekend, there was a pageant of boats on the Thames. Had we offered our continental friends a good seat to view the spectacle, they would certainly have declined **IF** – ... **(appall) CO** by the miserable weather forecast for the day. The English, however, showed their patriotism ... **(put up) CO** tents on the Embankment as early as 8 am. on Saturday, ... **RP** is a wonderful example of our willingness to defy* the elements.
But there are exceptions to this enthusiasm.
A carpenter ... **(live) CO** near Bury St. Edmunds commented upon the events as follows: "I do not understand what all the fuss is about. I couldn't care less. Just think of the costs. We could have invested the money in social welfare programmes." **RS** ... **(provide) CO** her health doesn't deteriorate over the next three years, Elizabeth II ... **MO** take Victoria's place as longest-reigning British monarch. Britain's head of state, ... **RP** came to the throne in 1952, has always tried ... **(steer) CO** clear of crises, ... **RP** has occasionally met with her subjects' disapproval. She did not sufficiently mourn Princess Diana's death in 1997, for example, and so people held a grudge* against her. **IF** Still, Elizabeth has always been a rock in a stormy sea ... **RP** waves drowned the marriages of three of her children.
Richard Foley from Sheffield, ... **RP** family faced poverty when he lost his job in a steel factory in 1987, ... **MO** start again from scratch. There was no steel industry left so he took up work as a mason*. **CO** He said, "She is an anchor. She gave her subjects support when Britain was in dire economic straits. Nobody ... **MO** accuse her ... **(be) CO** unconcerned about the welfare of her people." **RS**
... **(be) CO** described as an anchor ... **MO** be flattering to a charming elderly lady, to ... **RP** thousands of people paid homage* as the festivities came to an end. Despite the weather, the jubilee was a great success, even though the Duke of Edinburgh ... **MO** be admitted to hospital, ... **RP** was due to cystitis*. The crowd didn't cheer loudly enough, so the Queen's husband didn't hear them from his hospital bed. **IF**

* **infatuated** – vernarrt; **defy** – sich etwas widersetzen; **hold a grudge** – Groll hegen; **mason** – Steinmetz; **pay homage** – seine Ehrerbietung erweisen; **cystitis** – Blasenentzündung

C Beschreiben und benennen

10 Richtiger Umgang mit Nomen

Grundniveau

1 Countable and uncountable nouns →G77

Translate the following sentences in your exercise book. Decide if you need to use a countable or an uncountable noun. Sometimes the correct form might depend on the meaning!

1. Der Reiseführer gab uns gute Ratschläge und viele nützliche Informationen.
2. Möchtest du ein Eis? – Nur eine Kugel Schokoladeneis, bitte.
3. Immer mehr Leute haben immer weniger Zeit für ihre Hobbys.
4. Arzt: Gute Nachrichten: Sie brauchen nur Erholung* und Schlaf, um sich besser zu fühlen.
5. Viele Zeitungen sind auf Recyclingpapier gedruckt.
6. „Das Leben ist wie eine Schachtel Pralinen – man weiß nie, was man bekommt.“ *(Forrest Gump)*

2 Counting uncountable nouns – A recipe →G78

Read the following recipe for bread and butter pudding, a traditional and popular English dessert. Then answer the questions below.

Bread and Butter Pudding

Before you start make sure you have all the equipment you need: a pie dish, a saucepan, a baking bowl and a whisk* (or an electric mixer).

Here is the food you'll need for the ingredients: 50g butter, 10 slices of white bread (diagonally cut in halves), 50g raisins, 350ml milk, 50ml double cream, 2 large eggs, 25g sugar, a vanilla bean (or some vanilla extract), some grated nutmeg* and some cinnamon*.

Preheat the oven to 180°C. Grease* the pie dish with butter, spread each slice of bread with butter and cover the base of the pie dish with a layer of bread (buttered side up!). Sprinkle half the raisins evenly over the bread, then lightly sprinkle with a little nutmeg and cinnamon. Repeat this layer one more time or until the dish is filled.

Take the saucepan and heat the milk and cream gently. Take care that the liquid does not boil! Then beat the eggs in a large baking bowl with 3/4 of the sugar and the pulp* of the vanilla bean (or the vanilla extract) until the mixture is light and airy. Gradually pour the warm milk and cream over the eggs, beating all the time.

Pour the egg mixture slowly and evenly over the bread until all the liquid is added. With your hand gently press the bread down into the liquid. Sprinkle the remaining sugar over the surface, then leave it all to blend for 30 minutes.

Bake the pudding in the hot oven for 40—45 minutes until the surface is golden brown, the pudding has risen and the egg is set. Serve hot.

This recipe serves 4 people. It also tastes very good with custard*. Any leftovers? No problem: Cover the pie dish with some aluminium foil and reheat it in the oven.

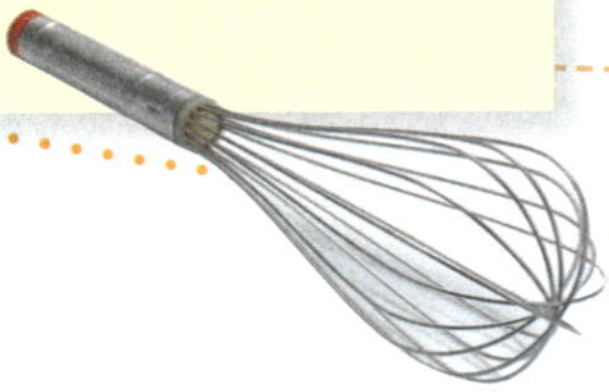

*Erholung – rest; **whisk** – Rührbesen; **nutmeg** – Muskatnuss; **cinnamon** – Zimt; **grease** – einfetten; **pulp** – Mark; **custard** – Vanillesoße

1. Which of the ingredients for the recipe are countable, which are uncountable?

countable: ______________________________

uncountable: ______________________________

2. Find two examples of a noun that is used as a collective noun (Sammelbegriff) and list the words in the text that each of these collective nouns stands for:

a) ______________________________

b) ______________________________

3. Find an example of a noun that is used as an abstract noun (abstrakter Begriff).

____

4. In the recipe the instruction is A: *Grease the pie dish with butter* .
There is a difference in meaning in this sentence: B: *Grease the pie dish with the butter* .

Tick the statement below that is correct. There might be more than one correct statement.

- ☐ A refers to some of the butter from the 50g in the recipe.
- ☐ A refers to all of the 50g butter in the recipe.
- ☐ B refers to some of the butter from the 50g in the recipe.
- ☐ B refers to all of the 50g butter in the recipe.
- ☐ Only A is logically correct, otherwise there would be no butter left for the slices of bread.
- ☐ Sentence B would also be logically correct in the recipe.

5. Why does the recipe tell us to bake the pudding until "the egg is set" when two eggs are used for the pudding?

- ☐ *The egg* here is used as a collective noun (Sammelbegriff).
- ☐ *The egg* here refers not to individual (countable) eggs, but to the mixture (uncountable) of beaten eggs blended with the sugar and vanilla.
- ☐ *The egg* here is used as an abstract noun (abstrakter Begriff).

6. Tick the sentences that are grammatically correct.

- ☐ For bread and butter pudding, you need a white bread.
- ☐ For bread and butter pudding, you need white bread.
- ☐ For bread and butter pudding, you need some white bread.
- ☐ Reheat the pudding in the oven using aluminium foil.
- ☐ Reheat the pudding in the oven using an aluminium foil.
- ☐ Reheat the pudding in the oven using some aluminium foil.

3 Plurals of nouns →G77–G79

a) *Choose the appropriate words to complete each sentence and put them in the correct form of the plural.*

formula · tooth · milk · belief · bread · father-in-law · Swiss · life · Dutchman · paper · fly · information · dice

1. We should respect people with different ________________ .
2. On board the aircraft were two ________________ and three ________________ .
3. Some men get on very well with their ________________ .
4. At the age of six most children start to lose their baby ________________ .
5. He handed in the answers to the exam questions on three ________________ .
6. The beach would be wonderful if it wasn't for those awful ________________ .
7. Many teenagers just don't know what to do with their ________________ .
8. These ________________ helped him to see the problem more clearly.
9. We can't play this game as you need two ________________ and we've only got one.
10. For cosmetics firms the ________________ for their products are top secret.
11. When you go shopping get two ________________ and four ________________ .

b) *Write down the correct form of the plural next to the singular. If no plural form is possible, write Ø.*

1. chair ________________
2. help ________________
3. sit-in ________________
4. candy bar ________________
5. ellipsis ________________
6. play ________________
7. man-teacher ________________
8. curriculum ________________
9. gold ________________
10. bush ________________
11. cash ________________
12. watercraft ________________

c) *Complete the sentences with an appropriate way of making the noun plural.*

1. They played him a ________________ music for his birthday on the radio.
2. That's a very good ________________ news!
3. Because it was so cold she gave him a ________________ soup.
4. I'll give you a useful ________________ advice.
5. You actually found your car keys on the beach. That was a ________________ luck!
6. For a dining room a table is a vital ________________ furniture.

4 Concord →G80

Read the following sentences and underline the form in brackets that you think is correct.

1. Either the Queen or her children (is/are) attending the ceremony.
2. It seems that neither the members of Parliament nor the Prime Minister (wants/want) to find a solution to the (problem/problems) the people have in (time/times) of financial crisis.
3. Ladies and gentlemen, the theatre is now open. We wish to remind you that everyone (has/have) to show (his/her/his or her/their) (ticket/tickets) at the entrance.
4. Teacher: OK, everybody, time's up. Put your (pen/pens) down on your (table/tables).
5. He was very shocked when he found out that his future wife had invited (his/her/their) sisters to (his/her/their) house without telling him – he had never met them before!
6. A huge variety of wines (is/are) on offer in this restaurant.

5 Collective nouns →G81

Fill in the correct singular or plural form of the verb in brackets, depending on whether it is appropriate in the sentence. You may also need to use the passive.

Example: Harvard ___is___ (be; simple present) one of the most respected universities in the United States.

1. The United Nations ________________ (try; present progressive) hard to come up with a joint resolution concerning the situation in the Middle East.
2. Microsoft ________________ (found; simple past) by Bill Gates in a garage.
3. Our school ________________ (win; present perfect) second prize in the national debating competition.
4. Our staff ________________ (vote; present perfect) to go on strike next Monday if the management ________________ (not make; simple present) a new offer.
5. In order to boost morale, the army fighting abroad ________________ (be; simple present) usually visited by the American President at Christmas.
6. The army ________________ (offer; simple present) career opportunities to lots of people that don't know what else to do.
7. Since the severe earthquake in 2011 that destroyed a nuclear power plant, the people of Japan ________________ (start; present perfect) to question the benefit of nuclear power.
8. Our team ________________ (tell; present perfect) that a talent scout from a well-known football club will be present during the match next week.
9. The press ________________ (regard; present perfect) as the fourth political force in the country since the 18th century.
10. Princess Diana died in a car crash in 1997. The press ________________ (pursue; past progressive) her all over Paris and unfortunately her driver was drunk.

6 Mixed exercise – Interpreting →G77–G83

Lindau on Lake Constance

Mona and Tim Schmidt were on a school trip to Scotland when they met Phil and became friends. Their parents invited Phil to stay for a few weeks during the summer holidays. As Mr and Mrs Schmidt can't speak English and Phil doesn't know any German, Mona and Tim have to act as interpreters. Today they are driving down to Lake Constance for the weekend.

Tell Phil what Mr and Mrs Schmidt are saying. Write in your exercise book.

1. Mr S: Diese Gegend hier heißt die Schwäbische Alb*. Das Gras an den Hängen ist so kurz, weil Schafe hier ständig weiden*.

Mona: …

Mr S: Wenige Touristen aus dem Ausland kennen die Gegend, weil wenig Werbung dafür gemacht wird.

Mona: …

2. Mr S: Diese große Fabrik gehört einer Firma, die exklusive Möbel herstellt.

Mona: …

Mr S: Das Management hat gerade angekündigt, dass sie expandieren wollen. Das ist eine gute Nachricht, weil es hier nicht so viel Arbeit gibt.

Mona: …

3. Mrs S: Hast du Hunger, Phil? Da sind ein Wurstbrot und ein paar Tomaten für dich. Außerdem habe ich Mineralwasser und Saft dabei.

Tim: …

Mrs S: Wir können bald eine Pause machen. Wir haben noch ein bisschen Zeit. Manchmal ist hier ein furchtbarer Verkehr.

Tim: …

4. Mr S: So, jetzt sind wir in Friedrichshafen. Die Franzosen hatten hier bis in die 90er Jahre eine Base.

Tim: …

Mr S: Die Stadt hat eine lange Tradition in der Entwicklung von Luftfahrzeugen und seit Neuestem bauen sie Teile von Raumfahrzeugen.

Tim: …

5. Mrs S: An der nächsten Kreuzung schau nach links, dann wirst du den See mit den Alpen im Hintergrund sehen.

Mona: …

Mrs S: Der See liegt auf der Grenze von Deutschland, Österreich und der Schweiz. Ungefähr 58 % des Sees gehören Deutschland.

Mona: …

Mrs S: Die Statistik zeigt, dass der Bodenseeraum immer beliebter wird.

Mona: …

6. Mr S: Schaut mal die ganzen Boote im Hafen! Man könnte fast meinen, dass hier jeder sein eigenes Boot hat!

Tim: …

Mr S: Durch das Wasser blendet* die Sonne so sehr. Willst du wirklich keine Sonnenbrille kaufen, Phil?

Tim: …

*__Schwäbische Alb__ – Swabian Jura; **weiden** – graze; **blenden** – dazzle

Aufbauniveau

7 Subjects composed of more than one noun →G84

Decide whether the following sentences need a singular or plural verb or whether both are possible. Tick where appropriate.

	singular	plural	both
1. *Tom and Jerry* (is/are) my favourite TV series.			
2. Tea and shortbread always (goes/go) together.			
3. Either English or French (is/are) compulsory in the finals.			
4. Salt and pepper (is/are) standing on the kitchen shelf.			
5. Mum and Dad (is/are) going to come home this afternoon.			
6. *Earth, Wind & Fire* (is/are) an excellent R&B band.			
7. Strawberries and cream (is/are) a must at Wimbledon.			
8. Both L.A. and San Diego (is/are) in California.			
9. Rings, flowers, a suit and a dress (is/are) needed for the wedding.			
10. Neither the butler nor the gardener (is/are) the murderer.			
11. Neither my friends nor my mother (knows/know) about this.			
12. The company's president or vice-president (is/are) going to speak at the conference.			

8 Compound nouns →G85

a) *These are definitions of which compound nouns?*

1. a library in a school: ______
2. a trip a class goes on with their teacher: ______
3. a bird that feeds on animals it attacks from the air: ______
4. an animation that is made with a computer: ______
5. some friends who know each other very well: ______
6. an auction at which (only) bikes are sold: ______
7. a web a spider tries to catch its prey in: ______
8. a leg of a chicken ready for a barbecue: ______

b) *Do the same task again. But be careful: Now you should pay particular attention to how the parts of the compound noun are joined and the way it must be written.*

1. a ticket a schoolchild uses to go to school for one season: ______
2. an auction at which a ten-year-old car is sold: ______
3. the mother of one's wife or husband: ______
4. the movement that fights for the rights of children: ______
5. the office in a town where residents can hand in their registrations: ______
6. a centre for communication in business: ______
7. a home where old people live: ______
8. a hill ants build in the forest: ______

9 A headmaster's speech →G86, G87

a) *A headmaster is preparing his speech for this year's graduation ceremony. Parts of the speech are still in note form. Use them to make statements with sentences as subjects, as in the example. Write in your exercise book.*

Ladies and gentlemen, dear graduates,

We are here tonight in order to award our graduate students their diplomas.

1. successfully passed their finals – great achievement!

That they have successfully passed their finals is a great achievement!

But tonight is not only the night they receive the diplomas they have been working so hard for over the last few years.

2. leave this school forever – tonight – means – new chapter in their lives will start
3. future – hold for them – unknown

I myself cannot say either. But I can tell them this:

4. not forget – dreams and hopes – this – key to success
5. am concerned about one thing in particular – their future lives

What will their lives be like in ten years time: Will they have completed their studies? Will they have found a decent job? Will they have started a family of their own?
In short:

6. will have succeeded in life? – something – I – happy to know

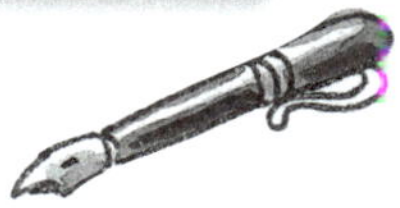

b) *The headmaster now wants to go on to talk about what some of the graduates are going to do after leaving school. Use the notes to make sentences with* **of***-expressions and other quantifiers in front of the subject, as in the example. Write in your exercise book.*

Every year I ask our graduates what they are planning to do after leaving school.

7. everybody says – going to go on holiday first of all

All (of) our students say that they are going to go on holiday first of all.

Why not? But what about the time after this well-earned break?

8. 80 of 120 students – graduating tonight – say – going to university

The remaining 40 pupils have arranged to start a training course.
Now, what does that mean? If you consider these figures, one thing is clear:

9. graduates – uncertain future – 0

This is a milestone for this school, of which we can be proud.

It means:

10. encouragement – staff/parents – not wasted

In the past students have regularly been graduating without any plans for the future.

11. last three years – such students (8, then 5, then 3) – decreased steadily

This year, finally, we have come to zero!
Congratulations on your decisiveness!

11 Pronomen

Grundniveau

1 Personal pronouns – You and "sie/Sie" →G88

a) *There are many ways in which **you** can be translated into German: Use the appropriate pronoun when you translate the following sentences and write them in your exercise book.*

1. Don't worry, Colin. The embassy will send you the visa before you fly to India.
2. Grandpa will tell you a bedtime story, children, if you brush your teeth and go to bed right now.
3. I can assure you, Ms Fisk, that you will receive the scholarship.
4. If you don't behave, Edwin, we will send you home to your parents on the next train.

b) *Likewise, "sie/Sie" (including the polite form of address) can be translated in many ways into English. Use the appropriate word when you translate the following sentences in your exercise book. (If you don't need an equivalent in English, put in Ø.)*

1. Sie ist unmöglich. Leute wie sie sollten nie Urlaub im Ausland machen.
2. Edna ist in Panik: Sie hat ihre Autoschlüssel verlegt und kann sie nirgends finden.
3. Ich mag die Geschichte nicht. Sie ist langweilig und unlogisch.
4. Trinken Sie eine Tasse Tee. Das wird Sie beruhigen.
5. Jemand hat ihre Katze vergiftet. Sie lag eines Morgens tot im Garten.
6. Zugegeben: Sie ist ein nettes Mädchen, aber willst du sie wirklich heiraten?
7. Uns gegenüber wohnen die Jacksons – kennen Sie sie? Sie sind gute Freunde von uns.
8. Es sind immer sie, die bis zum Schluss bleiben.

2 Personal, reflexive and reciprocal pronouns →G88, G90, G91

Decide whether you need a personal, reflexive or reciprocal pronoun or no pronoun at all (Ø).

Cathy will always remember __________ her first day as a young doctor in the casualty department. Naturally, __________ had not expected to enjoy __________ but so far __________ had prided __________ on her ability to remain calm in emergencies. After all, all the medical students had been trained to control __________ even in stressful situations. But this changed Ø radically that day. A little boy had cut __________ badly after running into a glass door. A very upset father had his small daughter with __________, who had scalded* __________ when a pot full of boiling water fell on __________. The father kept saying, "I'm so ashamed of __________. __________ should never have left __________ in the kitchen all by __________." The third case involved two men who had wounded __________ in a knife fight in a pub. Cathy felt like telling __________, "__________ have only __________ to blame. Why on earth did __________ go out with weapons on __________?" But then __________ said to __________, "__________ must remain objective and professional, Cathy. Pull __________ together, girl, put all this negative stuff behind __________ and just get on with the job."
So __________ kept these thoughts to __________. But at the end of the day, when all the casualty doctors were by __________, __________ complained __________ to __________ about the work of a hospital doctor.

*scald – verbrühen

3 Possessive, reflexive and reciprocal pronouns →G89–G91

Cross out the wrong word(s).

1. They adore Julia Roberts. In fact, they have always been great fans of her/hers.
2. Nobody will help her, so she will just have to rely on her/herself.
3. Solidarity among colleagues means helping one another/themselves.
4. Have you got enough money on you/yourself to buy a ticket?
5. Egoists are interested only in one another/themselves.
6. He took a quick look at him/himself in the mirror before shutting the front door behind him/himself.
7. I have no idea what her boyfriend looks like. Do you have a photo of him/his?
8. They were both still hungry so they helped themselves/each other to dessert from the buffet.

4 Demonstrative pronouns →G92

Put in the correct demonstrative pronouns.

1. Has there ever been a worse disaster in Japan than __________ of 2011?
2. I told her that her tattoo looked ugly. – __________ was very unkind of you!
3. __________ is my plan for this evening: a hot bath and an early night.
4. __________ who supported him when he needed them most were his true friends.
5. *(On the telephone)* Good morning, __________ is Mrs Parker. Is __________ Mr Pollock?
6. Who was __________ chatting with you for hours on the phone?
7. __________ really worries me: I work hard but my grades aren't getting any better.
8. Although I work hard my grades are really bad and __________ worries me.
9. Mmmm, your pies are so good. We should serve __________ at your party next week.

5 Indefinite pronouns I →G93

Fill in, choosing the suitable indefinite pronoun from the following:

somebody | everybody | something | anybody | nobody | anything | everything | nothing

When he was young and inexperienced, the boss of a small firm, Mr Parker, once made the mistake of assigning his staff a task without specifically saying who was to perform it.

The work, that of designing a flyer for __________ planning to open a shop selling organic food, was so easy that __________ in the office could have done it: there was not __________ in the least complicated about __________ like that. Unfortunately, however, __________ on his staff was rather lazy, so that __________ tackled the task and __________ whatsoever was done because __________ thought that __________ else would go ahead. Naturally, the result of this was that __________ ever got round to doing __________. When Mr Parker later enquired about the progress being made on the flyer, there was no reaction from __________. On realizing that they had not done __________, he was so furious that he wanted to fire __________ on the spot and, in future, do __________ himself. But __________ must have stopped him – maybe the awareness that he himself was partly to blame – so he decided to give __________ a second chance. From then on he always delegated __________ to __________ in particular, not to the staff as a whole.

6 Indefinite pronouns II →G93

a) *Complete the sentences with* ***some, any*** *or compounds with* ***some-, any-, every-.***

1. We seem to have run out of bread. Do you have ______________ ?
2. Did your mum bake some scones this morning?
   – Yes, she did. Would you like ______________ ?
3. Why are you so angry with Tom? – ______________ with a bit of common sense would have known how to react.
4. Well, thank you for coming here and telling us all about yourself.
   Now, is there ______________ you would like to ask us?
5. Sorry I can't help you at all. Why don't you ask ______________ else?
6. Why are you crying? Has ______________ awful happened?
7. I feel so stupid that I made that silly mistake.
   – Don't worry, ______________ could have mixed up the two bottles.
8. That man was the only one to boo.
   – Yes, ______________ else clapped and cheered.

b) *Choose the right pronoun and write it in the gap.*

1. Is Dick fond of his two daughters? – Very much so. He adores ______________ of them. either/both
2. All of Daniel's friends are British. ______________ of them is foreign. none/nobody
3. Both Jenny and Julia applied for the job but ______________ was successful. neither/none
4. Which of these two dresses should I wear tonight? – ______________ .
   There are equally pretty. either/both
5. There's no need to cry. ______________ will turn out well, believe me. everything/all
6. Here is some cake; please take ______________ . And there are also some ginger biscuits in that tin.
   Do help yourself to ______________ . a little/a few
7. I can't bear to read the newspapers any more. So ______________ of the news is bad. much/many
8. Does Penny collect autographs, too?
   – Oh, yes. But I don't think she's got as ______________ as you. much/many

7 Indefinite pronouns III – Missing Felix →G93

Complete, using ***some, any, some-, any-, every-, no-, each, all, none, both, either*** *or* ***neither.***

Two weeks ago Felix, aged 21, apparently vanished from the face of the earth, which has left all his best friends feeling very concerned about him. They are talking about his sudden disappearance.

Barbara: Have ______________ of you heard ______________ in the last couple of days?

Vanessa: ______________ at all, I'm afraid.

Trevor: I have just rung his parents but ______________ has had any news and ______________ are very upset. They are worried that ______________ terrible might have happened to him. It's strange that he went off without contacting ______________ of them.

Jeremy: ______________ told me that he had been talking of going to India.

Barbara: But surely he isn't the kind of person who would just take off without saying ______________ to ______________ of his friends or family?

Vanessa: Definitely not. ______________ might, but not Felix. So we can't just sit around doing ______________ at all. How about if ______________ of us start making enquiries in earnest?

Trevor: That's a good idea. If ______________ of us asks ______________ they know, we might learn ______________ useful. With a bit of information, we wouldn't feel quite so helpless.

Barbara: But what shall we do if there really is ______________ ? Then we will be back to square one.

Vanessa: Don't be so negative. At least then we will be doing ______________ . After all, ______________ , even if it's done in vain, is better than ______________ .

Trevor: That's true. And I can't believe that there is not ______________ whatsoever who has a clue as to his whereabouts. ______________ just vanishes into thin air unless they want to. So let's agree to do ______________ we can to find Felix. It's not as if our friend were just ______________ . On the contrary, he is ______________ who means a lot to ______________ of us.

Jeremy: OK, folks. Let's get ourselves organized. ______________ of you girls know a lot of his fellow students, so maybe you could ask ______________ of them. It shouldn't take too long if ______________ of you gets in touch with half of them. And ______________ Trevor and myself can make enquiries among his rugby mates. ______________ must know ______________ !

8 Interrogative pronouns →G94

Find and correct the mistakes in the following sentences. Put your corrections in the space between the lines.

1. What want you to be when you have completed your studies?
2. The shop assistant asked the customer what did she want.
3. How does the film star look? Is she slim, tall and dark-haired?
4. What is his favourite sport: swimming, jogging or tennis?
5. Who of them made that brilliant suggestion at the conference?
6. How is a female boar called? – A sow.
7. With who did he go to the party?
8. What does have the most calories: a burger or a tuna sandwich?
9. How are her prospects of a medal in the championships?

9 Possessive and demonstrative pronouns and the prop word *one* →G89, G92, G95

Fill in, using the most suitable pronoun or prop word.

The Williams family are sitting expectantly around the Christmas tree: the twins Barry and Ken, their sister Liz and their parents. Their cat Rosie and dog Rex are resting nearby, somewhat puzzled by these unusual goings-on. As the parents have been too busy to label the gifts, there is some confusion.

Dad: OK, folks, let's get the show on the road. I suggest the kids open ____________ first.

Liz: ____________ is a great idea, Dad. Now , let's have a look. Which ____________ is ____________ ?

Mum: Actually, you have more than one present, but do you see the flat parcel with the pink bow over there? It's one of ____________ . Unwrap ____________ first.

Barry: ____________ isn't fair. Why can't we boys open ____________ first?

Mum: Calm down, guys. ____________ big parcel here is for the two of you. You can open it while Liz is busy with ____________ .

Dad: And when you've finished with that lot, you can start opening the other ____________ that are in the corner. Ken, give Barry the small box, it's ____________ . The slightly larger ____________ is ____________ .

Mum: The square box in silver wrapping paper is for Dad. It's high time he opened one of ____________ .

Dad: What about you, darling? Take ____________ ; it's ____________ , with love from me.

(20 minutes later, surrounded by heaps of wrapping paper)

Barry: *(clutching his new computer game)*: Wow, ____________ is exactly the ____________ I wanted most. Can I try it out?

Mum: Why not? After all, it's ____________ now.

Ken: *(hugging his new basketball while studying the boxes with the twins' Lego spaceships)* ____________ look really fantastic. And the brand of my basketball is exactly the ____________ used in NBA matches. Super!

Mum: *(lovingly fingering the pearls of her new necklace)* Thank you, Dave. ____________ are the loveliest ____________ I've ever seen.

Liz: *(looking at her CDs and stroking her new cashmere sweater)* Mum, isn't ____________ the very ____________ we saw in that boutique window last week? I can't believe it's really ____________ . As for the CDs – how on earth did you guess that I wanted precisely ____________ ?

Dad: *(studying his sat-nav manual)*: Well, folks, if we get lost in future, the fault won't be ____________ but ____________ ! What a marvellous gift!

Mum: ____________ is what I'd hoped you would say.

Liz: Hey, we've forgotten Rosie and Rex!

Mum: Speak for yourself! There's a meaty bone in the fridge; ____________ is for Rex. As for Rosie, the tin of minced turkey is ____________ .

Dad: Well, guys, ____________ has been really fun and the presents are spot on*. It's clear that everyone is as pleased with ____________ as I am with ____________ . Why don't we do ____________ again next year? ____________ 'll be something to look forward to. Merry Christmas, everybody!

*be spot on – genau richtig sein

Aufbauniveau

10 English equivalents of the German "man" →G96

Choose the most appropriate way of expressing the German "man" when you translate the following sentences in your exercise book.

1. Man muss den Pass persönlich abholen.
2. Man plant eine Steuererhöhung auf Tabakwaren.
3. Als zuverlässiger Mensch darf man sein Wort nicht brechen.
4. Tommy, man sollte die Spaghetti nicht mit den Fingern essen.
5. Man sollte ihr die Wahrheit sagen.
6. Man hat mir gesagt, dass die Sitzung verschoben wurde.
7. Man weiß nie, ob er es ernst meint.
8. Man sagt, dass Kinder und Narren die Wahrheit sprechen.

11 Equivalents of the German "es" →G97

As you know, there are 4 ways of expressing the German "es" in English: ***it***, ***there***, ***so*** *and no equivalent (Ø). Translate the following sentences.*

a) **es – *it***

1. Wie weit ist es von Boston nach Chicago?

____

2. Es hängt alles davon ab, ob das Flugzeug pünktlich landet.

____

b) **es – *there***

1. Es müsste noch etwas Milch im Kühlschrank sein.

____

2. Es kommt eine Phase im Leben der meisten Menschen, wenn sie ein eigene Familie haben möchten.

____

____

c) **es – *so***

1. Wird Trixie mitkommen? – Ich hoffe es.

____

2. Während sie früher großzügig waren, sind sie es jetzt weniger.

____

d) **es – *Ø***

1. Wenn wir ihm nichts sagen, wird er es nie erfahren.

____

2. Der Prozess verlief so, wie wir es erwartet hatten.

____

e) ***Now you must find the appropriate equivalent yourself:***

1. Edgar zieht es vor, auf dem Lande zu wohnen.

2. Meinen Sie, dass es eine Zugabe* geben wird? – Ich glaube es nicht.

3. Anfangs ist es gewöhnlich schwer, sich an das Leben im Ausland anzupassen.

4. Es heißt in diesem Leitartikel* , dass der Präsident es in Betracht zieht zurückzutreten.

5. Der Nachmittagsunterricht fällt heute aus. Der Klassenleiter hat es soeben gesagt.

6. Wenn Kevin die Kamera nicht bedienen kann, musst du es ihm zeigen.

7. Es sieht so aus, als habe Nora ihre Verabredung vergessen.

8. Am Ende der Vorstellung gab es viel Beifall.

9. Wie viele Abgeordnete haben einen Sitz im Parlament? – Ich weiß es nicht.

10. Eveline ist schwanger. Ihre Freundin hat es mir erzählt.

11. Es besteht noch Hoffnung auf Rettung für die eingeschlossenen* Bergleute.

12. Es dauert etwa zehn Stunden, um nach Barbados zu fliegen.

*__Zugabe__ – encore; **Leitartikel** – editorial; **eingeschlossen** – trapped

12 Begleiter

Grundniveau

1 Definite and zero articles →G98, G99

Decide whether you need a definite article or no article (zero article: Ø) in the following gaps.

1. ___________ students have to pay high tuition fees in Britain and America. Fortunately, ___________ students who score top grades at ___________ university are sometimes awarded ___________ scholarships.
2. Sandra's parents were at ___________ school talking to ___________ headmaster on ___________ Wednesday when ___________ biennial fire drill took place.
3. Sam claims that ___________ money does not interest him whatsoever. Maybe that is why he seldom pays back ___________ money ___________ people lend him.
4. ___________ spring, ___________ summer and ___________ autumn were ___________ seasons when ___________ peasants used to have to work from ___________ dawn to ___________dusk.
5. My elderly uncle is usually at home in ___________ morning, except on ___________ Sunday, when he regularly goes to ___________ church.
6. A metal very much in demand nowadays is ___________ copper. In fact, ___________ copper used for ___________ cables supplying ___________ electricity to ___________ railway signals etc. is constantly being stolen.
7. If ___________ man does not start taking better care of ___________ environment, ___________ global warming and ___________ climate change could lead to ___________ extinction of ___________ life.

2 Definite and zero articles –Translation →G98, G99

Decide whether you need a definite article or no article when you translate these sentences in your exercise book.

1. Seit zwei Jahren lernt Lea in der Schule Gitarre.
2. Die englische Literatur erlebte im elisabethanischen England eine wahre Blütezeit*.
3. Da der Bäcker im Sommer immer im Morgengrauen aufstehen muss, macht er nachmittags gleich nach dem Mittagessen normalerweise ein Nickerchen*.
4. Wir dürfen die Hoffnung nicht aufgeben.
5. Das Leben macht nicht immer Spaß, vor allem wenn das Geld knapp* ist.
6. Die Hoffnung der Angehörigen* ist, dass das Leben des Vermissten noch gerettet werden kann. Aber die Zeit, die er schon allein und hilflos im Dschungel verbracht hat, ist einfach zu lang.
7. Wenn der Mensch die Natur liebt, muss er lernen, im Einklang mit der Umwelt zu leben.
8. Hast du vor, mit dem Bus oder mit dem Zug in den Urlaub zu fahren?
9. Welche der Gesetze, die in letzter Zeit vom Parlament verabschiedet wurden, hatten den größten Einfluss auf die Gesellschaft?
10. Warum hast du sein Geschenk auf dem Seeweg geschickt? Mit Luftpost wäre es viel früher angekommen.

*Blütezeit – heyday; Nickerchen – nap; knapp – tight; Angehörige – relatives

3 Definite and zero articles – Error spotting →G98–G100

The student who wrote these sentences in his essays put in the definite article wherever possible. He imagined that it was likely to be right at least half the time. Is this true? Find and cross out the mistakes he has made (sometimes more than one per sentence).

1. In the Victorian Britain the prudery was widespread, especially among the middle class.
2. The Princess Victoria was still very young when she ascended the throne and became the Queen.
3. Ronald was offered a place both at the Durham University and the University of Canterbury.
4. Barack Obama first stood for the president in 2008.
5. As a mark of the respect, the journalists were all asked to rise when the Pope entered the room.
6. The nasty Julian bullies the poor Max whenever the teacher leaves the room.
7. The construction of the castles proliferated in the medieval Europe, when the war was an integral part of the life.
8. The mountaineers Edmund Hillary and Tenzing Norgay were the first men to climb the Mount Everest.
9. No, they do not live in the High Street, their house is in the Chestnut Avenue.
10. The Colombian coffee is the favourite beverage of the Reynolds family.
11. The David Cameron you mean – the one who was elected the Prime Minister – is definitely not the David Cameron who went to the university with her.
12. The primates include such species as the monkey, the ape and the man.
13. When tourists visit London, they usually go (often by the Underground, also known as the Tube) to the sights which are most worth seeing like the Trafalgar Square, the Petticoat Lane, the Tate Gallery, the Hyde Park, the Buckingham Palace, the King's Road and the St Paul's Cathedral.
14. NASA is trying to measure the distance between the Mars and the Jupiter.

4 The indefinite article, the definite article used with adjectives and nouns →G101, G102

Write the translation of the following sentences in your exercise book.

1. Der Antiheld dieses Films ist Alkoholiker und Kettenraucher.
2. Als Armer kann er sich ein Studium an der Harvard-Universität nicht leisten.
3. Im Sommer hilft ihnen ein Arbeitsloser vier Mal im Monat im Garten.
4. Schweinebraten* wird es definitiv nicht geben, da der Ehrengast Jude ist, seine Frau Vegetarierin und ein anderer Gast Moslem.
5. Als alter Mann wurde Marvin zum Buddhisten.
6. Patrick ist Ire und Maria ist Portugiesin. Sie haben sich vor einem halben Jahr verlobt.
7. Als Anwalt, als Priester und als Arzt behandelt man Auskünfte immer vertraulich.
8. Ein Paar Socken als Weihnachtsgeschenk! Welch origineller Einfall!
9. Wie die Briten haben die Niederländer eine konstitutionelle Monarchie.
10. Die Wohlhabenden können sich mit den Problemen der Bedürftigen meist nicht identifizieren.*

*Schweinebraten – roast pork; sich mit ... identifizieren – to identify with

5 Mixed articles →G98–G102

Olga is Alice's Russian penfriend. As Olga's native language has no articles, she still has difficulty in using them correctly in English. For this reason she has decided to omit them altogether in her letter to Alice. Decide which articles are required in this excerpt from her letter. Where no article is necessary, write Ø.

I am having ________ lovely time in ________ United States. All ________ people I have met here have been so friendly. What ________ fascinating country America is! How fortunate as ________ nation ________ Americans are! Here is ________ brief summary of ________ things I have done so far: I have travelled on ________ steamboat down ________ Mississippi, hiked in ________ Yellowstone National Park, been given ________ autographs by some of ________ musicians playing ________ saxophone in ________ nightclub in ________ picturesque city of New Orleans, gone jogging on ________ shores of ________ Lake Ontario and even visited ________ Grand Canyon. Nothing ________ man has ever made can compare with what ________ nature has created there.

During my travels I have got to know ________ people from all over ________ world, for ________ example ________ Netherlands, ________ Mexico, ________ Iran and ________ Philippines. There was ________ nice girl from ________ Czech Republic who was in ________ US as ________ student at ________ University of South Carolina and who had to work as ________ waitress at ________ diner to earn some of ________ money she needed for her studies. One day she even got ________ tip of ________ hundred dollars from ________ particularly generous Texan.

Naturally, ________ life in "________ land of ________ free" has its downsides. On ________ trivial level, ________ food they serve in ________ restaurants I can afford is calorific and ________ American beer is not as tasty as ________ beer I am used to in ________ Europe. More importantly, not enough is done to protect ________ environment. But what I find most upsetting is ________ contrast between ________ lives of ________ poor and ________ luxury in which ________ rich live. This particularly struck me in ________ capital, where ________ Congress and ________ White House are ________ stone's throw from ________ ghettos inhabited by ________ underprivileged, where ________ hope of ________ better life has often been abandoned. If I were ________ politician, I would certainly try to narrow ________ economic gap between ________ disadvantaged and ________ well-to-do in ________ affluent country like ________ US. As ________ idealist, I refuse to accept ________ cynical view that ________ death is ________ only real democracy in ________ world.

6 Demonstrative and possessive determiners →G103, G104

Choose the correct word to complete each sentence. You may need to use some words more than once and other words not at all.

an **her** **his** **it's** **its** **one's** **ones** **that** **the** **their** **there** **these** **this** **those** **your**

1. ________________ chair over here is more comfortable than ________________ chair over there in the corner.
2. ________________ cereals up there on the top shelf are too high up for me to reach. I'll have to choose something from ________________ packets down here.
3. It's high time I did something about my bike. ________________ chain is too loose.
4. One should always put ________________ valuables in a locker for safe keeping.
5. ________________ a pity that she has broken up with her boyfriend.
6. Many young girls dream of having ________________ own horse.
7. The little boy had been stung in ________________ arm by a bee.
8. When we asked her for permission to leave, she nodded ________________ head.
9. ________________ used to be tinkers* travelling from village to village selling ________________ wares.
10. The Jewish men entered the synagogue with ________________ skull caps on ________________ heads.
11. Some hooligans were kicking an elderly homeless man in ________________ stomach.
12. Do you sometimes serve ready-made food or do you always cook ________________ own meals?

7 Quantifiers – Error spotting →G105

Find and correct the mistakes. Explain in German what the mistake was.

1. Nearly each member of the audience booed. ________________

   ____

2. All swimmers taking part in the next race are to start warming up. ________________

   ____

3. The maltreated child had bruises on every leg. ________________

   ____

4. These questions are so easy that every idiot could answer them. ________________

   ____

5. It took him much time to complete the Latin translation. ________________

   ____

6. They have far too few money to fly to Australia and back. ________________

   ____

7. Both cars are economical. Whichever you decide to buy, you will save money with each vehicle. ____________

   ____

8. Sam never bothers to vote, claiming each politician breaks pre-election promises. ________________

   ____

9. You seem to be having trouble with that. Can I give you any help? ________________

   ____

*tinker – Kesselflicker

8 Quantifiers – Saying it in a different way →G105

a) *Using **some** or **any** express the marked parts of the following sentences in a different way but without changing the meaning of the sentences. Use the word(s) in brackets and make any other necessary changes.*

Example: It doesn't matter what you give, it will be gratefully accepted. (donations/make)

Any donations you make will be gratefully accepted.

1. Are you thirsty? I can open a bottle of mineral water. (offer)

____

2. The police have no idea who knocked over the gravestones. (vandal)

____

3. Frank's party was a disaster. Only two guests turned up. (hardly)

____

4. No matter what meal you cook them, they will eat it. (food)

____

5. Have you run out of cheese? (Don't …)

____

6. Are you broke? I can help you out. (lend/money)

____

b) *Using **much**, **many** or **most**, do the same as in a). You will need to put any verbs in the right form.*

Example: Almost everyone will be watching the match this evening. (people)

Most people will be watching the match this evening.

1. Damian works too hard and he finds it difficult to keep up with his hobbies. (not have/time for)

____

2. The soup was terribly salty. (salt)

____

3. Our grandparents went to only few countries in South America. (not visit)

____

4. Her husband complains that she spends so much money on shoes. (buy)

____

5. Almost every German has learnt some English. (Germans/speak)

____

6. Candidates who are not charismatic have few supporters. (not have)

____

9 Quantifiers – Translation →G105

Write the translations of the following sentences.

1. Die beiden Schwestern sind ganz verschieden.

___

2. Sowohl Tom als auch Jerry bringen Kinder zum Lachen.

___

3. Sie müssen mit wenig Geld auskommen*.

___

4. Die beiden Kinder haben rote Haare, aber keins hat Sommersprossen*.

___

5. Die meisten Neuseeländer lieben Rugby.

___

6. Du hast zu wenig Pfeffer in die Suppe getan.

___

7. Ärzte in manchen Städten haben zu wenig Patienten.

___

8. Die beiden Bankräuber trugen Masken.

___

10 Interrogative determiners →G106

Underline the right word. More than one may be correct. If so, please explain the difference in meaning in your exercise book.

1. What/Which/Whose novel by John Le Carré do you find most fascinating?
2. What/Which/Whose animals are her favourite ones?
3. What/Which/Whose letter of the alphabet occurs most frequently in English?
4. What/Which/Whose explanation is more convincing, Sue's or Sandra's?
5. What/Which/Whose queen became Empress of India as well?
6. What/Which/Whose precious stone has she chosen for her engagement ring: a diamond, a ruby, an emerald or a sapphire?
7. What/Which/Whose name have they decided on for their baby?
8. What/Which/Whose planet in our solar system is closest to the sun?
9. What/Which/Whose parcel is this? Is it yours?

*auskommen – make do; **Sommersprossen** – freckles

Aufbauniveau

11 Mixed exercise – Error spotting →G107, G108

Find the mistakes in the following sentences and correct them in the space below.

1. Each other week they visit their grandparents.

2. All the human beings are descended from apes.

3. All except three of the passengers were injured.

4. Could you please buy a half pound of cheddar?

5. All six months Jane has her hair cut.

6. Each cat, whether large or small, belongs to the feline family.

7. You can visit us at every time that suits you.

8. We had never experienced a such catastrophe.

9. Every three-year-old could do that jigsaw puzzle.

10. Every guest at the party had brought a bottle of wine.

11. All people attending the trial were searched for weapons.

12. I think I have a flu. I am suffering from high temperature, headache and sore throat.

12 „Jede/r/s" und „alle" – Der Gourmet-Dinner-Club →G108

Translate the text in your exercise book.

Sie sind alle im Gourmet-Dinner-Club. Alle drei Wochen werden sie von einem anderen Mitglied eingeladen*. So muss jedes Mitglied nur etwa einmal im Jahr kochen und einmal im Monat essen alle Mitglieder ein köstliches Dinner. Dies gilt für* alle außer dem Gründungsmitglied, das als Belohnung für seine Idee nicht selbst kochen muss. Aber alle Köche zeigen gerne ihr Können* und das Gründungsmitglied ist zu jeder Zeit bereit, ein Dinner zu übernehmen, falls jemand kurzfristig* absagen muss. Jeder gute Koch könnte das machen, sagen Sie. Vielleicht, aber man muss schon mutig sein, schnell ein Gourmet-Dinner für ein Dutzend kritischer Köche herzuzaubern*. Jeder Koch will doch sein Bestes zeigen*.

*eingeladen werden** – (hier) be asked to dinner; **gelten für** – apply to; **Können** – (hier) skills; **kurzfristig** – at short notice; **herzaubern** – conjure up; **sein Bestes zeigen wollen** – want a chance to shine

13 Adjektive und Adverbien

Grundniveau

1 Adjectives – Attributive and predicative use →G109

a) *Find a suitable indefinite pronoun (**some-**, **any-** etc.) or adverb (-**where**) to go with the adjectives in the sentences.*

1. Employers want ________________________ punctual and reliable.
2. Most pensioners cannot afford ________________________ too expensive.
3. My friends would love to move to ________________________ vibrant and exciting.
4. Martin is very down-to-earth. He is interested in ________________________ remotely intellectual.
5. The director has not yet found ________________________ suitable for the role.
6. They were all very unhelpful. ________________________ present was willing to drive me to the station.

b) *Find a suitable adjective to complete the sentences. The marked parts will help you with the context.*

1. Sssh. The baby is ________________________ at last, thank goodness.
2. We met completely by chance. Our encounter was a ________________________ coincidence.
3. That man staggering out of the pub is obviously ________________________ .
4. Your dog scared the children and now I've got two very ________________________ little boys.
5. We've nearly finished the work on your car so you can collect it in the ________________________ days.
6. Half of the class didn't do any homework so the headmaster sent a letter to the parents of the pupils ____________ .
7. It was a mistake to serve free champagne as very soon a fight broke out between two groups of ________ students.

2 Translating adjectives →G109

Translate the following sentences.

1. Hör auf, du redest völligen Unsinn.

____

2. Du siehst krank aus. Fühlst du dich nicht wohl?

____

3. In den letzten Tagen war Frau Reynolds wegen ihres kranken Sohnes zu Hause.

____

4. Die für das Massaker verantwortlichen Soldaten wurden von einem Kriegsgericht verurteilt*.

____

5. Da Sarah vor Pferden Angst hat, will sie kein eigenes Pferd haben.

____

6. Die am Bombenattentat* beteiligten Terroristen sind nicht mehr am Leben.

____

7. Da Sams Kamera sehr alt ist, plant er nun eine digitale zu kaufen.

____

*__Schlägerei__ – fight; **verurteilen** – sentence; **Bombenattentat** – bomb attack

3 Comparison of adjectives and quantifiers →G110

Arnold is an above-average pupil in every subject except geography. Correct his mistakes in the following statements in two ways. If there is an adjective in the statement, use it in the correction.

Example:
Rainfall is heavier in Spain than in Ireland.

Rainfall is less heavy in Spain than in Ireland.

Rainfall is not as heavy in Spain as in Ireland.

1. The Danube is wider in Vienna than in Budapest.

   The Danube ________________

   The Danube ________________

2. The Nile is less long than the Rhine.

   The Nile ________________

   The Rhine ________________

3. London has fewer inhabitants than Birmingham.

   London ________________

   Birmingham ________________

4. Mount Everest is not as high as Mont Blanc.

   Mount Everest ________________

   Mont Blanc ________________

5. In Canada snowfall is less frequent than in Britain.

   In Canada snowfall ________________

   In Britain snowfall ________________

6. Coasts in Bangladesh are not as endangered by rising sea levels as those in France.

   Coasts in Bangladesh ________________

   Coasts in France ________________

4 Comparison of adjectives →G110

a) *Find the parts of the comparisons that go together and complete them by using a suitable adjective in the right form from the middle box. Write in your exercise book.*

1. Models are expected to be
2. Albert Einstein was
3. Advanced mathematics is
4. The Sahara Desert is

intelligent slim dry
complicated clever
large hard slender

almost all of us.
the Amazon rainforest.
is really healthy.
arithmetics.

b) *Find the parts of the comparisons from boxes 1, 3, and 4 that go together and complete them by using a suitable adjective or quantifier in the right form from the second box. Write in your exercise book.*

1. The earth is
2. With regard to health, milk is
3. A mechanic earns
4. Our village naturally has
5. Fossil fuels have a

far few
little
good
bad big
suitable

impact on the environment
from the sun
inhabitants
money
for children

than lemonade.
than the nearby town.
than renewable sources of energy.
than a bank manager.
than Mercury is.

5 Superlative adjectives →G110

Complete the sentences using the most suitable superlative form.

1. She has ______________________ outlook on life possible. (positive)
2. Giving that film an award was ______________________ decision. (controversial)
3. They displayed ______________________ behaviour ever seen at a football match. (brutal)
4. He didn't want to go to the concert, which was ______________________ . (strange)
5. After ______________________ wait we had ever had our plane finally took off. (long)
6. He said he would follow her over ______________________ mountain and across ______________________ ocean. (high, deep)
7. The gradual change of mood during the play was ______________________ . (subtle)
8. Our team lost 2:1 after extra time, which was ______________________ result. (disappointing)

6 Superlative adjectives and quantifiers →G110

In your exercise book write sentences, using the most appropriate superlative adjective or quantifier.

1. Monthly salary

2. A level French results

3. Flying distance from Manchester Airport

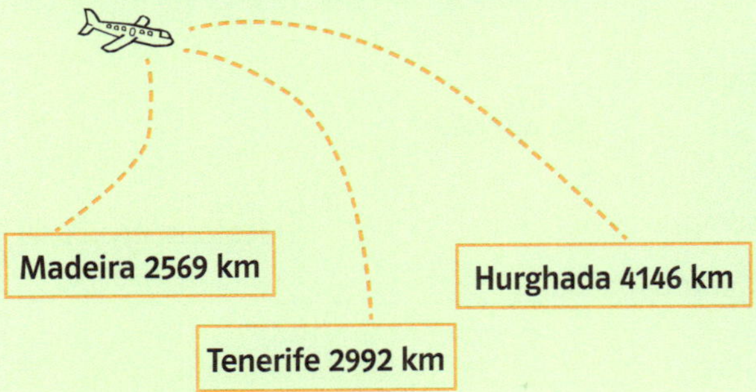

4. Results of poll on how people rate animals' intelligence

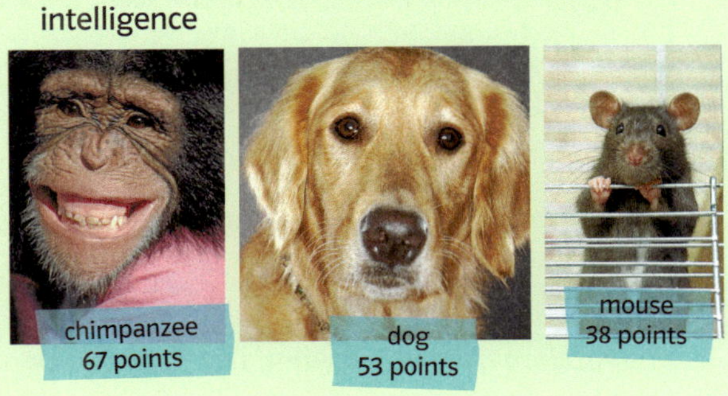

5. population

6. The Jonas Brothers

7 Comparison of adjectives, participles as adjectives – Error spotting →G110–G112

Find and mark the mistakes in the text. Then correct them in the spaces between the lines.

I am visiting the famous artist in his gallery in New York, in one of the exclusivest parts of Manhattan.

He is feeling very annoying as he has just received some disappointed news. With the economic situation becoming always worse an exhibition has been cancelled.

He shows me his latest work: an installation in which a blind is collecting donations from door to door in a wealthy suburb. No one gives him anything. Of all his later work I find this the less easy to understand.

He explains: It's a political statement showing how the rich ones choose to ignore the problems of the poors.

Farther information about his latest work will be revealed in a three-part documentary later this year, called "Artist: the lonelyest profession of the world."

The door opens and his brother and sister come in. His brother, Alfred, is three years elder than him.

He is also more tall then his brother. Jane is perhaps a year younger and intensely shy, the shiest person I have met in a long time.

8 Adverbs →G113

a) *Cross out the wrong words.*

1. Professor Smithers listened **patient/patiently** to what the student was saying.
2. Our hosts welcomed us very **friendly/amiably**.
3. My brother tasted the oyster soup extremely **sceptical/sceptically**.
4. On the whole the weather was **fair/fairly** good.
5. That mushroom omelette tasted **wonderful/wonderfully**.
6. Stop acting so **silly/foolishly**!
7. Mary found Sandra's unkind remark about her new jeans **most/mostly** upsetting.
8. Sally is not a serious person. In my view, she tends to take things too **light/lightly**.

b) *Use the right word from each pair to complete the sentences.*

1. How ________________ did the pupils perform in the oral exams?
   Amalie felt ________________ in her new dress. **good/well**
2. Simon looked ________________ at the gang of hooligans approaching him. **nervous/nervously**
   As the gang had knives and baseball bats, it's no wonder Simon looked ________________.
3. The inhabitants of the Fukushima region were hit particularly ________________ by the tsunami.
   The inland regions were ________________ affected by the tsunami. **hard/hardly**
4. You're right, Dave has been ________________ depressed over the past few weeks.
   Then they arranged the flowers ________________ in several vases. **pretty/prettily**
5. I haven't seen her ________________ so I don't know how she is.
   They're very busy so he's been getting home ________________ a lot. **late/lately**

9 Adverbs and functions of adverbs →G113, G114

Translate the following sentences in your exercise book, paying special attention to the marked parts.

1. Der Präsident hat den Raum gerade betreten.
2. Unser Neffe wurde zu Unrecht des Diebstahls angeklagt*.
3. Es kann zu Recht behauptet werden, dass in jenem Land die Opposition grausam unterdrückt wird.
4. Obwohl Susie gerne Filme anschaut, liest sie [doch] lieber Romane.
5. Vermutlich wird James weiter nach einem geeigneten Arbeitsplatz suchen.
6. Schließlich fanden wir die alten Fotos zufällig auf dem Dachboden.
7. Vielleicht wird die Rezession bald vorbei sein, aber viele Experten meinen, sie könnte noch länger andauern.
8. Ehrlich gesagt, fühlten wir uns absolut enttäuscht.

10 Comparison of adverbs and quantifiers →G115

Form comparative and superlative adverbs and quantifiers from the adjectives in brackets.

Last week's soccer match was particularly thrilling, with a resounding 6:1 victory for our team. Alex, our top footballer, played __________________ (brilliant), even __________________ (good) than usual. Despite not scoring any goals himself, Terry played __________________ (reliable) and worked __________________ (hard), always ready when needed. Brad, a born athlete, ran __________________ (fast) and kicked the ball __________________ (far), in fact __________________ (far) than ever before. Patrick's passes were always perfect; after all, he is the one who invariably passes __________________ (accurate). The moment we fans enjoyed __________________ (much) was naturally the one the opposing team liked __________________ (little): it was when Alex kicked the ball between the goalposts just two minutes into the match. Never has our team scored __________________ (early) than that! This swift goal demotivated our opponents so much that they played __________________ (little and little) __________________ (confident). They ran __________________ (slow), passed __________________ (precise) and, all in all, performed __________________ (bad) than any other premier league team I have ever watched.

11 Position of adverbs →G116

a) *Error spotting. Find and underline the misplaced adverbs, then rewrite the corrected sentence in your exercise book. Be careful: not all of them are in the wrong position.*

1. The police have been already informed about the attempted assassination.
2. A new law was yesterday passed by Parliament.
3. In order to see better she took forward two steps.
4. Before you start using appliances, you must read the instructions carefully.
5. If you faster run, you might catch your bus.
6. Since the Norman Conquest Britain has been never invaded.
7. The conference begins tomorrow at 9 o'clock.
8. Recently a delegation of French industrialists visited China.
9. Have there been lately any remarkable developments?
10. Floods cause frequently serious damage and loss of life.

*des Diebstahls angeklagt – accused of theft

b) *Put the adverbs in the right place in the sentences and write the sentences in your exercise book. Sometimes more than one solution is possible.*

1. We must finish our work. today
2. Children prefer junk food to healthy meals. often
3. Travelling long distances by ship is necessary today. rarely
4. Can the effects of global warming be observed? everywhere
5. The protesters believed in the success of their joint efforts. firmly
6. Our committee meets. every fortnight/on Tuesday/in the town hall
7. We have got petrol to reach the next filling station. enough/hardly
8. The meeting will take place. soon

12 Adjectives and adverbs →G109–G116

Complete the text, using the appropriate adjectives and adverbs (sometimes comparative or superlative) and other words from the selections below. Where necessary, form adverbs from the adjectives. Some words may be used more than once.

Ancient Civilisations

1. It is ______ knowledge that, dating back to 8000 B.C., Jericho is the ______ city ______ the world. Its walls were ______ built around 6000 B.C., and since then it has had many as they have ______ been destroyed during its history. What is less ______ known is that a ______ ______ culture existed in the Indus Valley between 2500 and 1600 B.C. in the region of ______ Pakistan. The cities ______ vanished without trace long ______, but while they existed their civilisation was ______ advanced ______. Their citizens even created their ______ writing, which was roughly ______ old ______ the hieroglyphic script of the ______ Egyptians. What is even ______ were the sewers they constructed to remove ______ waste and ______ water from houses. These cities remain ______ to this day as there is ______ any archaeological evidence that could provide ______ information.

2. ______ Athens is ______ for being the birthplace of democracy because political decisions ______ were made ______. ______, its democracy functioned ______ from democracies ______. The ______ difference is that ______ ______ men had civil rights. Women and slaves were ______ not treated ______.
______ Rome, with one million inhabitants, was the ______ city ______ the world in those times. It was ______ a kingdom, then a ______ republic and ______ an empire. Its ______ emperor was ______ Julius Caesar, who became emperor in 44 B C. For the next ______ centuries the empire was ruled by means of ______ rather than civil power. After being divided into two parts under Diocletian, it was ______ reunited under Constantine, the ______ emperor to adopt Christianity ______.

1. ago, amazing, ancient – as, common, developed, extreme, far – first, frequent, good – hard, high, human – in, mysterious, old – own, present-day, technological, there – used

2. ancient, collective, different, equal, famous – few, final – first, free – in, large, military, natural, obvious, official, only, probable, self-ruling, temporary, there – thus, today, well-known

Aufbauniveau

13 Compound adjectives →G117

Translate in your exercise book, using compound adjectives to express the marked words in English. Use the expressions from the examples in your grammar book or ones similar to them.

1. Familie Butler verbrachte einen unvergesslichen – ja einmaligen – Urlaub in Schottland.
2. Megan hat dunkelrotes Haar und tiefgrüne Augen.
3. Wir brauchen Statistiken, die auf dem neuesten Stand sind.
4. Dieser Computer ist auf dem neuesten Stand der Technik.
5. Die Polizei darf keine Auskünfte über laufende Ermittlungen geben.
6. Pass auf – das Wasser ist kochend heiß!
7. Opas Ansichten über die Gleichberechtigung sind ziemlich altmodisch.
8. In diesem Restaurant gibt es nur glutenfreies Essen.

14 Compound adjectives and forms of adverbials →G117, G118

a) *Write sentences using the information given. Form compound adjectives by combining the marked words. Decide whether you need one word, two words or hyphenated adjectives.*

1. The coastal regions of both Bangladesh and the Netherlands lie low.

   Both ______________________________

2. Our uncle died last week. He was 79 years old.

   Our ______________________________

3. Janet's face was so pale that we were afraid she was going to faint.

   Janet ______________________________

4. Ugh! The water in the pool is so cold it could freeze. You should have warned me!

   Ugh! You should ______________________________

5. The honeymooners thoroughly enjoyed their cruise in the Caribbean. It lasted three weeks.

   The honeymooners ______________________________

6. Your jog was 20 kilometres long. Aren't you absolutely exhausted?

   Aren't you ______________________________

b) Write sentences using the information given and using the underlined words to form adverbials.

1. You can imagine my astonishment. She passed her exams!

   ____

2. I needed an answer. Because I was so impatient I decided to call the next day.

   ____

3. Now that her suitcase was unpacked she went down to the hotel swimming pool.

   ____

4. They went home early so that they would avoid the rush-hour traffic.

   ____

14 Aussagen gewichten

Grundniveau

1 Emphatic *do* I →G120

Put stress on the marked verbs by using a **do***-construction. Mind the tense.*
a) *Write in the spaces between the lines.*
b) *Then translate each sentence into appropriate and idiomatic German in your exercise book.*

1. Patrick doesn't read a lot. But he buys two Sunday papers every weekend.
2. I quite agree. Thomas looked rather depressed the other day.
3. You needn't remain standing all the time. Please take a seat.
4. I knew the weather was about to change but I didn't expect such a thunderstorm.
5. Stop making such a noise!
6. Crossing the border, Miss Hillman knew she had nothing to declare but she felt somewhat nervous when the customs officer asked her to open her suitcase.
7. Mr Gray was not sure whether he could make it but he managed to attend the meeting after all.
8. The Fukushima disaster makes you wonder about the hazards of nuclear power.

2 Emphatic *do* II →G120

Simon's mother is giving him a good telling-off. As Simon considers her reproaches unfair, he uses the emphatic **do** *in his replies. Complete his answers to the accusations, using the verbs on the right.*

1. Mother: You hardly ever clean your room. It's a real pigsty.
   Simon: I ______________________ it, only not as often as you'd like. **clean**
2. Mother: Your friend Geoffrey never takes off his trainers when he lies on your bed.
   Simon: That's true, but he ______________________ that they're clean. **make sure**
3. Mother: You didn't bother to visit Grandma in hospital last Sunday.
   Simon: I ______________________, but the visiting hours were over. **go**
4. Mother: I don't think you spend enough time revising for exams.
   Simon: I ______________________ enough time – look at my good grades! **spend**
5. Mother: You didn't remember to buy Dad a Father's Day present.
   Simon: I ______________________, but the book I ordered was out of print. **remember**
6. Mother: Your girlfriend never says hello to me when she drops by.
   Simon: She ______________________ you. It's just that she mutters a bit because she's shy. **greet**
7. Mother: Well, maybe you could be right.
   Simon: I am right. I ______________________ you're being overcritical at the moment. **think**

3 Emphatic expressions →G121

Jill inclines to understatement whereas Marilyn tends to exaggerate. Complete Marilyn's emphatic way of expressing Jill's more hesitant statements, using the following words:

grossly **just the** **totally** **thorough** **utter** **sheer** **single most** **very own** **whatsoever**

1. **Jill:** The Sistine Chapel in Rome is quite nice, isn't it?
   Marilyn: Nice? Its ______________________________ beauty is breathtaking!
2. **Jill:** Marion isn't very intelligent.
   Marilyn: You can say that again. She's a(n) ______________________________ idiot!
3. **Jill:** I'm not too keen to go to choir practice today.
   Marilyn: Nor am I. In fact, I have no desire ______________________________ .
4. **Jill:** Brad Pitt is a good-looking guy, don't you think?
   Marilyn: Are you kidding? He's the ______________________________ handsome man on earth!
5. **Jill:** Miriam isn't exactly thin, is she?
   Marilyn: Not thin? She's ______________________________ overweight!
6. **Jill:** My brother's bedroom is a bit untidy.
   Marilyn: What are you talking about? It's in a ______________________________ mess.
7. **Jill:** The Thompsons seem to be quite wealthy.
   Marilyn: That's for sure. They even have their ______________________________ indoor pool.
8. **Jill:** The teacher didn't explain those algebra equations very well.
   Marilyn: His explanation was worse than useless. It left me ______________________________ confused.
9. **Jill:** I wouldn't fancy eating snails, with or without butter and garlic.
   Marilyn: Don't even mention them! ______________________________ idea makes me sick.

4 Emphatic expressions – Translations →G121

Translate in your exercise book, paying special attention to the marked emphatic expressions.

1. Auf gar keinen Fall würde er einem Wildfremden Geld leihen.
2. Tonys Kollegen waren überrascht, dass ausgerechnet er Gruppenleiter geworden war.
3. Sie finden jede erdenkliche Ausrede für ihre schlechten Noten.
4. Seine einzige Tochter ist die alleinige Erbin* seines Nachlasses*.
5. Stell dir vor: Er hatte seinen Pass verlegt, seine Fahrkarte vergessen und – zu allem Überfluss – seine Brieftasche verloren.
6. Warum um alles in der Welt wurde das Gemälde für nur $800 verkauft, obwohl der tatsächliche Wert viel größer war?
7. Viele Menschen interessieren sich nicht im Geringsten für Literatur.
8. Als er krank war, hat ihm der bloße Gedanke an Essen den Magen verdreht.
9. Obwohl unser Arbeitgeber einige Bedenken* hat, besonders was die Kosten angeht*, unterstützt er grundsätzlich unser Projekt.

*__Erbin__ – heiress; **Nachlass** – estate; **Bedenken** – reservation; **was … angeht** – as far as … is/are concerned

5 Emphatic *do* and emphatic expressions →G120, G121

Olivia and Angus are talking to their son, Sandy (21), about his planned holiday in New Zealand.

Make their conversation more emphatic by forming constructions with ***do*** *in 8 suitable places and using the following emphatic expressions:*

perfectly | of all times | very | whatsoever | utterly | sheer

Find the places, mark them and write the emphatic expressions in the spaces between the lines

Angus: Of course I am aware that earthquakes are relatively rare in New Zealand but they sometimes happen.

Olivia: And when an earthquake occurs, such as in Christchurch in 2011, the results can be horrifying. Just think of the number of casualties!

Sandy: I know all that. After all, I watch the news, too! Besides, my Kiwi friend Malcolm described the disaster in great detail in his emails. But surely there won't be one during my stay!

Angus: I hope you are right.

Olivia: But be careful, dear. We want you back in one piece. The thought of something terrible happening to you worries me sick. You know we love you very much.

Sandy: There's no reason to get upset, Mum. I can assure you that I am capable of looking after myself. Remember: you brought me up to be independent!

Aufbauniveau

6 Constructions with *there* →G122

There are many ways in which *there* is used at the beginning of a sentence or phrase to emphasise the meaning. By no means all of them can be translated as "es gibt …".

Translate the following sentences, trying to find the most appropriate German equivalent for the ***there****-construction. Write in your exercise book*

1. Is there anything wrong with the TV?
2. There were a lot of patients sitting in the waiting room.
3. There used to be a dairy shop at the corner of Melville Street.
4. We are sure there must be a better way of dealing with that difficulty.
5. There comes a point when you have to make a decision.
6. There remains the question of who is going to pay the bill.
7. There is no doubt that momentous decisions lie ahead for the new government.
8. He is so unpredictable that there is no knowing what he will do next.
9. There have been many questions asked about the president's background.
10. There are so many sights to see in Venice.
11. There is no denying the fact that smoking is bad for your health.
12. Once upon a time there was a king who had three daughters.

7 Partial inversion →G123

You have had an unpleasant experience at the supermarket and are telling some friends about it. Since it happened to you, you want to tell the story in an interesting way so you use partial inversion for the purpose of emphasis. George, an acquaintance who helped you out, has a more matter-of-fact way of saying what happened.

Write your story in the first person in your exercise book.

Example: He had no idea what lay in store for him. Little did I know what lay in store for me.

He was about to pay the checkout operator when he realized he was in a fix.
He searched for his wallet without success. It was nowhere to be found.
The customers in the queue were frowning and muttering so impatiently that he became really nervous. He had seldom felt so embarrassed.
His desperation was growing to such an extent that he wanted to take to his heels.
Just as he contemplated flight, he heard a familiar voice – mine.
He had rarely felt so relieved to see a friendly face.
As soon as I realised what a predicament he was in I offered to pay his bill.
He has learnt one thing from this experience: he will under no circumstances go shopping again without his wallet.
But he never wants to show his face there again.

8 Inversion and partial inversion – The Forbes Expedition →G122, G123

The following text is an excerpt from the logbook of an expedition into the heart of Sumatra in the late 19th century. The style is very factual. Make it more dynamic by using inversion and partial inversion. The marked parts of the text indicate where you can make improvements. Write the whole story in your exercise book.

Examples:
The record of the first day of our expedition follows here.
Here follows the record of the first day of our expedition.
This was the only place where nature showed her beauty in such profusion.
Nowhere else did nature show her beauty in such profusion.

We did not know when we set out at the break of dawn that this would be a momentous day. The snow-capped peaks and volcanoes of the mountain ridge stretched away in the distance. The vast expanse of rainforest which we had to penetrate before reaching the waterfall, our destination, lay between them and us. No European had ever beheld that as yet uncharted waterfall.
The native scout, equipped with a sharp machete, who cleared the path through the seemingly impenetrable jungle, marched at the front of the group. Alexander Forbes, the leader of the expedition, followed hard on his heels. His native servant Amir, who was carrying his rifle and constantly watching out for danger, strode beside him. Tigers might be lurking in the depths of the jungle, ready to attack the unwary [There...]. A variety of specialists made up our team of explorers. Forbes did not just have the good fortune to have the support of biologists but also of a geographer, a botanist and a photographer. A host of sturdy native porters walked at a steady pace at the rear. Though their loads were heavy, they seemed to carry them with ease.
After several hours of arduous marching Forbes suddenly stopped and listened alertly. He smiled. His ears had not been playing tricks on him at all. The thunder of a mighty waterfall came unmistakably through the cries of the birds and animals. He peered through his binoculars, but however hard he tried, he was unable to make out anything because the green foliage of the forest was so dense. The expedition continued until, to our amazement, the jungle opened before us and a spectacle that took our breath away appeared there. The destination of our expedition and the fruit of all our efforts lay in front of us.
A deafening roar came out of the mist. The mighty masses of the river plunged down into a pool white with foam. Even though we were exhausted, we stood motionless in inexpressible awe, drinking in the view for some minutes. We had just congratulated each other when it was time to settle down to our work. Many tasks had to be performed [There...]: in addition to having to determine our exact position and taking as many photographs as the dwindling light would allow, we had to rest our weary limbs and have food prepared and tents erected for the night. Days of observation and documentation of the landscape's distinctive features as well as its flora and fauna lay ahead of us eager scientists. We could hardly wait to begin our work the very next day.

9 Cleft sentences →G124

a) *Rewrite the following sentences, adding emphasis by using an* ***it****-construction.*

1. Everybody was taken by surprise by what the magician did next.
2. Agatha Christie wrote "The Mousetrap".
3. The last straw breaks the camel's back.
4. At the airport Mr Miller realized that he had left his passport at home.
5. The worst damage was done when the tsunami struck the coast.
6. I got a phone call from my friend in Tokyo only yesterday.
7. The fire broke out just after midnight.
8. Mrs Hamilton was not able to attend the meeting because she had broken her leg the day before.

b) *Rewrite the following sentences, adding emphasis by using a* ***what****-construction.*

1. Mr Wallace is interested in prehistoric burial sites.
2. Caroline didn't know how to restart the computer.
3. First we will make a plan.
4. I like Susan but I disapprove of the way she dresses.
5. You need to fill in this questionnaire.
6. This study is dealing with the possibilities of conserving energy in industrial production.
7. The bad acoustics of the new concert hall disappointed me.

8. Desmond was working at his thesis when his computer crashed.

c) *The following sentences can be turned into both an* ***it****- and a* ***what****-construction. Write both versions and note the difference in meaning.*

1. Keeping your self-control is what matters most.

2. I can't understand how Sarah can put up with her moody husband.

3. What people will think of him worries him most of all.

4. Conservative investors appreciate the relatively stable value of gold.

5. I am looking for the new edition of Shakespeare's complete works.

Focus C

1 The social effects of the Industrial Revolution on South Wales →K11–K13

Complete the text, using
– an article AR *(sometimes you have to decide if you need one at all),*
– an adjective or adverb AD *(Under each part there is a list of adjectives in the sequence they appear in the text. You may need a comparative or a superlative.),*
– a quantifier QU*, – a determiner* DE*, – a pronoun* PR*.*

1. QU__________ Briton with a sense of AR_____ justice must have felt AD______________ appalled on reading AR_____ results of AR_____ "Commission of Enquiry into the State of Children in Employment" in the 1840s. AD________________ the AD________________________ revelation in DE___________ report was that, in QU__________ – though AD______________ not QU__________ – cases AD________________ children or PR__________ who were even AD______________ were toiling in coal mines.

utter **probable** **distressing** **fortunate** **five-year-old** **young**

2. AR_____ situation in Merthyr Tydfil in South Wales is AR_____ classic example of AR_____ conditions AD__________________ in AR______ iron works and AR______ mines. The Dowlais iron works there were the AD__________________________ PR__________ in the world in the first half of the 19th century, exporting AR_______ products such as AR_______ rails to Russia and countries even AD________________ away. Being so close to AR_____ iron ore, AR______ coal, AR______ limestone and AR______ water, Merthyr Tydfil was the AD___________ location for iron works of DE_________ kind. As AR_____ result of DE__________ circumstances, Merthyr Tydfil had become the AD_________________ town in Wales by 1851 and grew even AD________________________ when coal mining south of the town began.

prevailing **productive** **far** **ideal** **large** **populous**

3. It was a very AD___________________ age for AR_____ owners of AR_____ mines and iron works in South Wales. However, while AR_____ rich became AD______________________________________ the situation of the workers and DE_________ families grew AD_________________________________ As wages were reduced AD_________ whenever AR_____ price of AR_____ iron or AR_____ coal fell, AR_____ poverty was widespread.

profitable **wealthy** **miserable** **frequent**

4. Furthermore, being paid by results, miners had to work extremely AD___________ and AD___________ for twelve or more hours AR_____ day. In spite of PR_________ , AR_____ average weekly wage of AR_____ adult colliers* was only 70p. PR_________ was considered not QU__________ AD____________ than AR_____ slavery. For a family to survive, QU__________ parents as well as QU__________ of their AD____________ children had to work. In addition, the miners QU__________ had to pay two and a half pence AR_____ week for their AD___________ lights. QU__________ child labourers were carried into the mine shafts by DE_________ fathers, but they were AR_____ lucky PR_________ ; PR_________ of them had to climb down the AD_________________ ladders by PR__________________ .

hard **fast** **good** **old** **own** **dangerous**

5. The workers could not afford houses of their AD___________ , so that PR__________ were often three to four families living in a small cottage. As working women and girls had very QU___________ time for housework, in QU__________ cases AD_______________ QU___________ time at all, the AD_______________ conditions were AD_______________ shocking, leading in AR_____ summer to outbreaks of cholera like PR___________ of 1849. Having to work from AR_____ dawn to AR_____ dusk or even AD___________ , only very QU___________ children were able to go to AR_____ school. Therefore PR___________ were numerous families in which PR__________ of the members could read or write.

own | hard | sanitary | absolute | long

6. AD_______________ , since DE__________ "bad old days" PR___________ has been done to improve the situation of PR__________ still working in mines. For example, the AD_____________ idea of AR_____ child labour is now unthinkable in AR_____ UK and modern miners very AD_____________ die at AR_____ work. Nevertheless, even today a QU___________ parts of Merthyr Tydfil are still AD___________________________ disadvantaged. In 2006 DE__________ city was described as the third AD_______________ place to live in Britain, only slightly AD_____________ than two areas of London.

obvious | mere | rare | economic | bad | good

2 Error spotting →K10–K14

Find and mark all the mistakes in the following text, then write the corrected version in your exercise book.

The Whistler

Celia left the house, not in hurry. She heard the door snap shut behind herself and turned right. It was getting darkly and ahead a ten-minutes walk to the nearer bus-stop lay. Leisurely she walked down the trees-lined street with the odd car parked alongside the kerb on every side.
When she glanced at a shop's window, Celia caught sight of her mirrored in the dark glass. She liked that which she saw. Her makeup seemed perfectly and she was wearing the new lowly cut dress she had bought recently herself for that occasion, not the one her mother had advised her to wear. Would Oliver like it so many as she did? He had wanted always herself to look prettily. You are my sweetheart, he would say, and he would hold her in two arms and kiss her tender on her lips. Did he truely love her? Never she would forget what he had whispered in her ear the other day…
The street was absolute empty now. Only three more blocks she had to walk before she could feel safely in the bus.
Suddenly heard she anybody whistling. It was a weird and haunted tune. She turned round but couldn't see somebody. Unwitting she quickened her pace. An icily shudder ran up the spine. Her mind raced. Could it be he, the Whistler? What had the radio report said? "Over the last weeks the news have been full of that mysterious killer. Its been the talk of the town. He has strangled already few women at dusk in deserted streets. The police has not been able to catch him already. At no time somebody has seen him; the only thing known about him is that a strange whistling has been heard near the scene of crime short before any horrifying passer-bys stumbled upon the unfortunately victim."
Celia tried hardly to run but the legs refused to obey. She felt paralysing. Her heart was in the mouth, beating frantic. There was anybody to whom she could turn for a help.
Now she could hear even hasty steps. They were coming always closer to herself. She froze with fear. She imagined strong gloved hands around the neck. Despite her terror she turned and near fainted: Oh, Oliver, she thought …

D Review

15 Übergreifende Übungen

1 Penny Lane →K1, K2, K7, K9, K10, K12, K13, K14

Penny Lane was one of the biggest hits by the Beatles in the 1960s. Written by John Lennon and Paul McCartney, it focuses on a street in the Beatles' hometown Liverpool.

In Penny Lane there is a barber showing photographs
of every head he's had the pleasure to have known.
And all the people that come and go
stop and say hello.
On the corner is a banker with a motorcar,
the little children laugh at him behind his back.
And the banker never wears a mac*
in the pouring rain – very strange.

Penny Lane is in my ears and in my eyes,
there beneath the blue suburban skies
I sit, and meanwhile back

In Penny Lane there is a fireman with an hourglass*
and in his pocket is a portrait of the Queen.
He likes to keep his fire engine clean,
it's a clean machine.

Penny Lane is in my ears and in my eyes,
a four of fish and finger pies
in summer, meanwhile back

Behind the shelter in the middle of the roundabout
A pretty nurse is selling poppies* from a tray.
And though she feels as if she's in a play
she is anyway.

In Penny Lane, the barber shaves another customer,
we see the banker sitting waiting for a trim.
And then the fireman rushes in
from the pouring rain – very strange.

Penny Lane is in my ears and in my eyes,
there beneath the blue suburban skies
I sit, and meanwhile back
Penny Lane is in my ears and in my eyes,
there beneath the blue suburban skies.
Penny Lane

Take a close look at the song and do the following tasks. Write your answers in German in your exercise book.

1. *Line 1:* Replace the participle with an equivalent construction.
2. *Line 3:* Which past tense is used in this clause? What is its function and why is it impossible to use the simple past?
3. *Line 3:* "… he's had the pleasure to have known" is called a "contact clause". Make a relative clause instead and explain the difference between the two options?
4. *Line 3:* "pleasure" is an "abstract" noun, which usually doesn't require an article. Why is it used here?
5. *Line 5:* You can use an inifinitive or a gerund construction after "stop". Which of these constructions means the same as "stop and say hello" and what would the other construction mean in the context of the song?
6. *Line 6:* In this clause the subject comes after the verb (inversion). Why is it done here? In similar cases in the song, which different construction is used?
7. *Line 8:* Explain the use of the simple present.
8. *Line 15:* Would there be a difference in meaning if a gerund instead of an infinitive clause were used here?
9. *Line 15:* You might expect to find an adverb "cleanly" after the verb "keep". Why is an adjective used here instead?
10. *Line 19:* Could you use the definite article in front of "summer" without altering the meaning?
11. *Line 21:* Explain the way the plural "poppies" is made.
12. *Line 24:* Why is the simple present used here and not the present progressive?
13. *Line 27:* Why does the verb "rushes" end in "-es"?

*__mac__ – Regenmantel; __hourglas__ – Sanduhr; __selling poppies__ – Jeden Herbst werden Mohnblüten aus Papier verkauft, um Geld für wohltätige Zwecke zu sammeln.

2 Trouble at school →K2, K4, K5, K6, K7, K12, K13

a) *In the following text deal with these tasks:*

V : *Put the given verb in the correct tense.*
Sometimes you may need a passive construction.
AD : *Decide if you need an adjective or an adverb.*
GI : *Decide if you need a gerund or infinitive clause.*
RS : *Put direct into reported speech.*
DC : *Replace the parts in italics with a different construction.*
Decide if you need:
– a particple clause
– a gerund clause
– a sentence relative clause
– a shortened relative clause

Two students, Brad and Todd, V ________________ (sit) in the principal's secretary's office. DC *As they didn't know what was in store for them,* ____ , they were a little worried. Todd V ________________ (be) wise enough GI ________________ (take off) his baseball cap, whereas Brad didn't seem to be afraid GI ________________ (make) a bad impression on the principal and V ________________ (keep) his cap on.

Both students V ________________ (look) AD ________________ (anxious) at a huge sign RS which said "please wait to be yelled at". ____ .

RS Brad asked Todd: "Do you really think she will yell at us?"
____ Todd replied: "I'm afraid so.
We V ________________ (not/stuff) all of the toilet paper down the toilets."
____
____ . But they V ________________ (be) unlucky and their class teacher V ________________ (catch) them.

The secretary, Mrs Palmer, V ________________ (not notice) that the boys were nervous. She V ________________ (stare) at her computer screen and V ________________ (torture) the keyboard. AD ________________ (apparent), she was quite indifferent to the boys' fate. She was doing her job DC *and that* V ________________ (expect) *of her*, ________________________ . As for the principal, Mrs Fiorinello, she V ________________ (sit) at her desk V ________________ (study) AD ________________ (careful) the report DC *which had been written* ________________ by the boys' class teacher.

DC *Because the door to her office was wide open* ________________________________ the boys could see her and she V ________________ (look) AD ________________ (pretty) AD ________________ (angry). She was dressed in black and for Brad and Todd, DC who were ________________ for her verdict, this was a bad omen.

b) *What sort of punishment do you think would be appropriate for Brad and Todd? Think of five different punishments. You will need to use modal verbs.*

____
____
____
____
____

3 T.C. Boyle: The Tortilla Curtain

In *The Tortilla Curtain* Cándido and his young wife, América, come as illegal immigrants from Mexico to the United States. Their dreams of finding work and a better life in California are not realised. The following excerpt is taken from the end of the novel and describes how a flood causes their world literally to collapse around them.

And so, in the end, it all came tumbling down on Cándido: his daughter's affliction,the pelirrojo with the gun, the very 1 mountain itself. The light was flickering 2, the rain hissing like a box of serpents prodded 3 with a stick. She can't see, Cándido, she can't see anything 4, América said, and in that moment he had a vision of his perfect plump little daughter transmogrified 5 into an old hag with a cane and a Seeing Eye dog, and before he could assimilate the meaning of all that in all its fearful permutations and banish it from his consciousness, there was this maniac with the gun, 6 threatening his life, and before he could even begin to deal 7 with that, the mountain turned 8 to pudding, to mush, the light failed 8 and the shack fell 8 to pieces. At first he didn't know what was happening 9 – who would 10? – but there was no resisting that force 11. He could have built his shack of tungsten steel with footings a hundred feet deep and the result would have been the same. 12 The mountain was going somewhere, and he was going with it.

T.C. Boyle, *The Tortilla Curtain*, 1995

tumble - *fall*
affliction - Leiden
pelirrojo - Rothaariger
flicker - flackern
prod - anstupsen
transmogrify - verwandeln
permutation - Umsetzung
hag - *ugly old woman*
hiss - zischen
banish - verbannen
mush - Brei
shack - *small hut*
tungsten - Wolfram
serpent - *snake*

The numbers in the text refer to the tasks below. Write your answers in your exercise book.

1 Where, in a sentence, would you normally expect to find the word "very"? How is it used here in the text? What is its function and how would you translate "the very mountain itself" into German?
2 What tense is used here? Could the simple past be used here? Would it make a difference in meaning?
3 Define the verb form. Rewrite the clause employing a different construction.
4 Is it possible to replace "anything" with "something"? Explain why (not).
5 Use a relative clause instead of the past participle.
6 Explain why the omission of the comma would change the meaning of the sentence.
7 Would it make a difference in meaning if one used a gerund instead of an infinitive construction?
8 Explain the use of the simple past.
9 Explain the use of the past progressive.
10 Finish the sentence that starts with "who would". How else can "would" be used? Make sentences to demonstrate these uses.
11 Rewrite the clause in two ways. For one use an active and for the other a passive construction.
12 Rephrase the whole sentence using a conditional clause.

4 Error Spotting – First draft of a "Facharbeit" →K1, K2, K4, K5; K7–K13

The following text is the beginning of a "Facharbeit". The student gave this first version to the tutor, who noted where corrections needed to be made.

Use the tutor's notes to correct the mistakes and write the corrected version in your exercise book.

passive genitive passive type of noun
Before we investigate the social problems of America today I think it's necessary to give a few general
informations:

construction construction pronoun
The USA is a country that is situated in North America and is comprising 50 states. With it's population
type of noun preposition
of 313 million peoples it is the third largest country of the world both by land area and population. The
pronoun gradual increase word order!
number of inhabitants is getting each year ever larger.

genitive numbers! tense numbers!
In 1980 the USA's population was 226 millions and in the year 2008 it has already been 304 millions. It is
construction not adjective tense adverb
interesting noting that the number of Americans over 75-years-old increases continuous since 1980 and
numbers! concord construction
now more than 13 millions Americans are over 75, those are 4.1% of the population. By the population
article compound noun pronoun article
growing the expectancy of life has also gone up. One explanation for this facts might be that the modern
form of modal verb type of noun commas tense
medical science could develop better treatments for diseases. A man, who had died of cancer 20 years
passive
ago, advances in medical care can now cure, for instance.

passive word order indefinite pronoun indefinite pronoun
We see the USA often as the country where all is possible. All have heard the expression "The American
indefinite pronoun relative pronoun
Dream", but not all in America can live this dream. Who doesn't know the story of the dishwasher which
article construction modal verb article
ended up as millionaire? Instead that they live this dream, many must live with a unemployment rate of
plural ? adverb
8.2 per cents, the highest one since 25 years.

adjective as noun superlative with time
What might be the reasons for the increase in unemployeds during the last years? The beginning of this
comma! relative pronoun tense quantifier
phase might be found in the finance crisis of the year 2007, what then has affected each sector of the
determiner
economy. At this time unemployment became the number one issue for millions of Americans. A poll in
concord construction
February 2009 showed that 47 per cent of respondents was afraid to lose their job, whereas 65 percent
tense
were knowing someone who had been laid off.

article compound adjective type of clause tense
As example, take Duane Simmons, a 62 years old mechanic, who has worked for the same company
adverb determiner register
in Ohio since 33 years, almost the entire life. One day the company for which he worked was bought
style relative clause passive word order
by another company, what didn't worry Mr Simmons at first, but then they closed quickly
genitive passive type of noun preposition
the company of Mr. Simmons down. You can find many more informations about cases like this in the
internet.

5 Mediation – Healthy school meals →K1–K6, K8, K9, K12, K13

Die Fritten-Revolte

Weil ihnen das gesunde Kantinen-Essen nicht passt, proben britische Mütter an der Highgate Comprehensive School den Aufstand und liefern ihren Kindern Fast Food ans Schultor. Sie ärgern sich darüber, dass ihre Kinder in der Mittagspause ausschließlich gesunde Kost vorgesetzt bekommen. Aufgerufen zu der Kehrtwende hatte der bekannte Fernsehkoch Jamie Oliver. Vor allem das fettige Essen der Schulkantinen, sei schuld daran, dass britische Kinder die dicksten in ganz Europa seien. Also stellte die britische Regierung 20 Millionen Pfund bereit und ließ Pommes und Burger weitgehend von den Speiseplänen verbannen. Stattdessen gibt es neuerdings viel Gemüse, Obst und gesundes Essen wie Fisch. Auf wenig Verständnis stießen die Mütter bei Schulleiter John Smythe. Das gesündere Schulessen würde zwar nicht bei allen Schülern gut ankommen, hätte aber bereits positive Auswirkungen gezeigt, sagte Smythe. „Die Kinder lernen jetzt nachmittags viel besser."

This report appeared in a German newspaper. At that time you were on a school exchange in England, not far from the school mentioned in the article. You conducted an interview with the headmaster for your school newspaper but the recording didn't work.

Fortunately you made notes in German so now you can use them to reconstruct the interview. The grammar and vocabulary notes on the right will help you write a full interview.

Grammar and vocabulary notes:

1. (Stell dich vor, Frage an den Direktor (John Smythe): Hintergrund der Kampagne, Initiator.)

tense, polite question – modal
Initiator: use a verb here, tense

___

2. (Direktor: Jamie Oliver (berühmter Koch): zu viele Kinder zu dick, falsch ernährt. Änderung möglich durch gesünderes Mittagessen an Schulen, an seiner Schule umgesetzt.)

reported speech, tense, quantifier
falsch ernährt: use an active verb
if-clause, passive
passive

___

3. (Frage: Unterstützung durch Regierung, welche?)

Unterstützung: use a quantifier in English
interrogative pronoun

___

4. (Direktor: gab 20 Millionen Pfund, neue Richtlinien fürs Schulessen erlassen.)

£20 Mio: say more about purpose
passive

___

5. (Frage: bedeutet ‚Pommes und Hamburger verbannt?)

tense, passive,
verbannen – *banish*

6. (Direktor: ja, gutes Beispiel von Schule erwartet, nur gute Ratschläge reichen nicht, jetzt viel frisches Essen – Gemüse, Obst, wenig Fett.)

passive, infinitive construction, type of noun
reichen – *be enough*
Essen: *food* or *meal*?
quantifier

7. (Frage: Welche Reaktionen von Schülern und Eltern?)

tense
Reaktion: use a verb, interrogative pronoun

8. (Direktor: neues Essen nicht bei allen beliebt. Mütter begannen, in Mittagspause Fast Food an Schule zu bringen.)

active sentence, tense
sequence of adverbs
article

9. (Frage: Meinung zur Aktion der Mütter?)

Aktion: use relative clause with *what*

10. (Direktor: versteht die Aktion nicht, sehr schlecht, weil Mütter Gesundheit der Kinder gefährden; werde etwas dagegen unternehmen müssen)

tense
gefährden – *endanger*
tense

11. (Frage: Was genau?)

tense

12. (Direktor: Schule bietet weiterhin gesundes Essen an; Gespräch über Sache mit Eltern suchen. Mütter müssen dann aufhören, sonst Polizei holen und verhaften lassen)

tense, construction (gerund/infinitive)
tense,
Gespräch: use a verb
if-clause
German "lassen"

13. (Danke für das Gespräch)

gerund construction

Text- und Bildquellenverzeichnis

Textquellen:

7: 3 *The Story of an Hour* © Kate Chopin 1894; **15: 6** Excerpt from *The Road Home* by Rose Tremain, Vintage Books, London, 2008 © Rose Tremain 2007; **18–19: 9** Excerpt from *Man Proposes … from Campbell's Crossing And Other Very Short Stories* by Alan Maley, Penguin Books Ltd, London, 1995 © Alan Maley1995. All rights reserved; **22–23: 4** Excerpt from *Educating Rita: A Comedy (Acting ed.)*, by Willy Russell, Samuel French Ltd, London, 1981 © Willy Russell 1981. All rights reserved; **36: 1** Excerpt from *Waiting for Sunrise* by William Boyd, Bloomsbury Publishing, London, 2012 © 2012 by William Boyd; **53:8** Excerpt from *Stone Cold* by Robert Swindells, Hamish Hamilton, London, 1993 © Robert Swindells 1993. All rights reserved; **114: 1** "Penny Lane" Text: Lennon, John/McCartney, Paul © Sony-ATV Tunes LLC, Sony/ATV Music Publishing (Germany) GmbH, Berlin; **116: 3** Copyright © 1995 by T. Coraghessan Boyle, permission by Mohrbooks AG, Zürich

Bildquellen:

1.1 shutterstock (Yuri Arcurs), New York, NY; **4.1** Fotolia.com (Robert Kneschke), New York; **4.2** MEV Verlag GmbH, Augsburg; **5.1** Thinkstock (istockphoto), München; **5.2** Mauritius Images (Mode Images), Mittenwald; **8.1** iStockphoto (Kirsty Pargeter), Calgary, Alberta; **10.1** Franziska Rosentreter, Hamburg; **12.1** Thinkstock (iStockphoto), München; **15.1** Corel Corporation Deutschland, Unterschleissheim; **17.1** Picture-Alliance (EPA/Kerim Okten), Frankfurt; **21.1** Getty Images (Hiroshi Higuchi, Photolibrary), München; **22.1** ddp images GmbH (Jadis), Hamburg; **26.1** akg-images, Berlin; **26.2** Fotolia.com (Platinum Pictures), New York; **26.3** Punch Limited, London; **26.4** shutterstock (Becky Stares), New York, NY; **26.5** shutterstock (Richard Sargeant), New York, NY; **27.1** Thinkstock (iStockphoto), München; **27.2** NASA (PD), Washington, D.C.; **28.1** shutterstock (Yampi), New York, NY; **29.1** Inge Voets, Berlin; **29.2** Klett-Archiv, Stuttgart; **32.1** iStockphoto (letty17), Calgary, Alberta; **32.2** Fotolia.com (Maria Brzostowska), New York; **33.1** Corbis RF, Düsseldorf; **33.2** iStockphoto (Simon Smith), Calgary, Alberta; **33.3** shutterstock (Paul Shlykov), New York, NY; **34.1** Avenue Images GmbH (Stockbyte), Hamburg; **35.1** shutterstock (Stuart Miles), New York, NY; **35.2** Klett-Archiv, Stuttgart; **38.1** Cinetext GmbH, Frankfurt; **39.1** Thinkstock (istockphoto), München; **39.2** iStockphoto (Mark Aplet), Calgary, Alberta; **41.1** Fotolia.com (Nuryudijes), New York; **41.2** shutterstock (Sergey Lavrentev), New York, NY; **41.3** iStockphoto (tempurasLightbulb), Calgary, Alberta; **41.4** shutterstock (Dmitriy Shironosov), New York, NY; **43.1+2** Thinkstock (istockphoto), München; **44.1** Fotolia.com (Luki Schelbi), New York; **45.1** shutterstock (Kiselev Andrey Valerevich), New York, NY; **46.1** shutterstock (Bikeworldtravel), New York, NY; **48.1** Alamy Images (Jack Sullivan), Abingdon, Oxon; **50.1** iStockphoto (Woodstock), Calgary, Alberta; **52.1** shutterstock (nld), New York, NY; **55.1** shutterstock (Michelle Brown), New York, NY; **56.1** shutterstock (StockLite), New York, NY; **58.1** shutterstock (Simon Krzic), New York, NY; **59.1** iStockphoto (Stephen Rees), Calgary, Alberta; **59.2** shutterstock (Bikeworldtravel), New York, NY; **62.1** Alamy Images (RF Kase), Abingdon, Oxon; **62.2** shutterstock (Baloncici), New York, NY; **65.1** Fotolia.com (Carmen Steiner), New York; **65.2** shutterstock (Viktor1), New York, NY; **69.1** Fotolia.com (helix), New York; **70.1** Getty Images RF (PhotoDisc), München; **71.1** iStockphoto (Giorgio Fochesato), Calgary, Alberta; **71.2** Corel Corporation Deutschland, Unterschleissheim; **72.1** Thinkstock (istockphoto), München; **74.1** Klett-Archiv, Stuttgart; **74.2** shutterstock (Joy Brown), New York, NY; **75.1** Alamy Images (David Grossman), Abingdon, Oxon; **76.1** Thinkstock (George Doyle), München; **77.1** shutterstock (Zoran Karapancev), New York, NY; **77.2** Verena Ballhaus, München; **77.3** shutterstock (Richard F. Cox), New York, NY; **78.1** Thinkstock (istockphoto), München; **78.2** Fotolia.com (blue eye), New York; **78.3** Fotolia.com (Paylessimages), New York; **79.1** Thinkstock (Photodisc), München; **79.2** Ingram Publishing, Tattenhall Chester; **79.3** iStockphoto (RF), Calgary, Alberta; **82.1** iStockphoto (Dlugoska), Calgary, Alberta; **84.1** Elsie Lennox, London; **85.1** Fotosearch Stock Photography (PhotoDisc), Waukesha, WI; **86.1** MEV Verlag GmbH, Augsburg; **87.1** shutterstock (Robyn Mackenzie), New York, NY; **88.1** shutterstock (Eduard Kyslynskyy), New York, NY; **92.1** shutterstock (Fara Spence), New York, NY; **93.1** Fotolia.com (Thomas Faivre-Duboz), New York; **93.2** Klett-Archiv (Marion Rausch, Frickenhausen-Linsenhofen), Stuttgart; **94.1** dreamstime.com (Czuber), Brentwood, TN; **97.1** Avenue Images GmbH (imageshop), Hamburg; **97.2** shutterstock (Jeff Lim C.W.), New York, NY; **97.3** Avenue Images GmbH (image 100), Hamburg; **100.1** CC-BY-SA-3.0 (Verbund Österreichische Elektrizitätswirtschafts-AG); **100.2** shutterstock (Pichugin Dmitry), New York, NY; **100.3** Fotolia.com (minicel73), New York; **101.1** Fotolia.com (Jason Stitt), New York; **101.2** shutterstock (William Perugini), New York, NY; **101.3** dreamstime.com (Joy E. Brown), Brentwood, TN; **101.4** Thinkstock (Digital Vision), München; **101.5** Thinkstock (istockphoto), München; **101.6** Fotosearch Stock Photography (Maps Resources), Waukesha, WI; **101.7** shutterstock (Featureflash), New York, NY; **103.1** creativ collection Verlag GmbH, Freiburg; **105.1** Fotosearch Stock Photography (Brand X Pictures), Waukesha, WI; **109.1** ddp images GmbH (Thomas Lohnes), Hamburg; **110.1** MEV Verlag GmbH, Augsburg; **111.1** Thinkstock (istockphoto), München; **111.2** iStockphoto (Bonnie Schupp), Calgary, Alberta; **113.1** MEV Verlag GmbH, Augsburg; **114.1** shutterstock (Matt Hart), New York, NY; **115.1** www.CartoonStock.com (McPherson, John), Bath; **116.1** iStockphoto (Mel Stoutsenberger), Calgary, Alberta; **118.1** iStockphoto (RF), Calgary, Alberta

Sollte es in einem Einzelfall nicht gelungen sein, den korrekten Rechteinhaber ausfindig zu machen, so werden berechtigte Ansprüche selbstverständlich im Rahmen der üblichen Regelungen abgegolten.